A Gentle Architecture

François Spoerry
A Gentle Architecture

from Port-Grimaud to Port-Liberté

introduction by Marc Gaillard

translated from French by
Madeleine Masson

with a Foreword by
H.R.H. The Prince of Wales

Pheon Books
in association with
John Wiley & Sons Limited
Chichester ● New York ● Brisbane ● Toronto ● Singapore

credits

This book in the English language is based the edition first published in French by Robert Laffont, Paris, under the title *L'Architecture douce, de Port-Grimaud à Port-Liberté.*

The French and English editions were served by Mireille de Mun as editorial consultant.

The lay-out was designed by Maxence Scherf.

Published by Pheon Books, an imprint of Carden Publications
limited, in association with John Wiley and Sons, in 1991.
Distributed by John Wiley and Sons Ltd., Baffins Lane, Chichester, P019 1UD, England.
© 1989, Robert Laffont S.A.
© 1991, François Spoerry.
© 1991, Madeleine Masson for the English text of this edition.
All rights reserved. Printed in France.

acknowledgments

The author would like to thank Madeleine Masson for her friendly advice and excellent translation; Mireille de Mun for her collaboration and efficient work to have this book published.

When I was serving in the Royal Navy in 1971, based at Toulon, I remember seeing a village being built near the port of St Tropez. It was Port Grimaud. I recall then thinking how wonderful it was, but it was only recently I learnt that the architect was François Spoerry.

I found that this book – with its illustrations of Port Grimaud and projects of similar charm – raised my spirits, as well as my admiration for the achievements of the architect responsible. I sincerely hope it proves to be a useful contribution to the growing movement concerned with reintroducing traditional values and principles into urban design.

Contents

Foreword by H.R.H. The Prince of Wales 7
A Passionate Architecture, an Introduction by Marc Gaillard 11
Towards a Gentle Architecture 17
Myths of Modern Architecture 25
The Art of Living 29
A Swamp in the Bay of St Tropez 33
A Reassuring Architecture 47
The Elements of a Gentle Architecture 57
Achievements of Modern Architecture 60
Architecture, A Most Public Language 65
Dreams and Realities 69
A Great American Project 102
Architecture Regained 120
Chronology 124
Index to the photographs and illustrations 127
Notes and incidental remarks 127
Credits 128

Architecture with a Passion

He has a frank, open countenance which inspires instant liking. His glance is both candid and humorous. A ready smile hovers about his mouth. His voice is deep and well-modulated and his whole attitude friendly and welcoming. It is immediately obvious that this man's life has been out of the ordinary. He seems to look benevolently on humanity in general, and it is evident that very early on he acquired the equilibrium which has made him into the astute and balanced person he is today.

François Spoerry's innate modesty inhibits him from talking about himself. He is happier talking about his passionate interests: his large yachts and his battles for architecture. In order to understand what lies behind this unpretentious and courteous facade, it is important to see this man in framework of the family home in Mulhouse. Built in the last century by his great-grandfather, one of the greatest and most powerful of the cities industrial magnates, the house is set in a park shaded by centuries-old oaks, sun-dappled beeches and majestic cedars, it is situated on a hillside overlooking the city. Built in the English style of the late XIXth century when great store was set on both comfort and solidity. It is obvious from François Spoerry's deep attachment to his family home that it was from this house and from his native city that he drew so many of the spiritual and moral values which have governed his life.

It was here in Mulhouse, in 1945, that François Spoerry opened his first and principal office which still houses his oldest colleagues. It was on the drawing-boards here in the rue-Sainte-Catherine that so many of the projects have been conceived – among them the plans for Port Grimaud and some of those for Port Liberté.

Though he has chosen to live at Port Grimaud increasingly in the course of the last dozen years, it remains Mulhouse through which one can best understand the powerful traditions from which François Spoerry has welded both his passions and his actions.

It shows him to be worthy successor to generations of Spoerrys characterised by their dedication to hard work and perseverance in whatever task they undertook. These family traditions, however, are sufficiently flexible as to be spiced with a taste for adventure as well as the need for interaction.

These are the spurs which have activated François Spoerry and forced him to become a perpetual nomad, the victim of the immense success of his ideas and his projects. So frenetic and peripatetic are his life and activities, that he can never spend more than a few days at a time at either his family home in Mulhouse or at the beautiful but spacious house that he has built at Port Grimaud opposite the harbour entrance, at the point where the harbour subdivides into the canals at the very end of the peninsular known as the "Ile Longue". This spacious house, which combines the best features of both Southern and traditional French architecture is built, as they say, between the courtyard and the garden. It exemplifies Port Grimaud and is at the same time a brilliant example of the *gentle architecture* François Spoerry so extols. Welcoming, warm and unpretentious the house seems indistinguishable from all the others built at Port Grimaud other than that it is larger and that it is dominated its Saracen tower. Light reflected from the waters of the harbour floods in through the plate glass windows of the facade. At the very heart of the large sitting room water, itself, is used in the form of a pool separated from the swimming pool in the garden by a plate glass window whose lower lip is flush with the surface of the water. One only need dive underneath the window to pass in, or out, of the garden. This original and amusing detail is again symbolic of both water and of François Spoerry's lagoon city. The inclusion of water within the house is again underlined by the boat house built under the Saracen tower, which makes it possible to disembark in the shelter of the great watery porch onto the landing stage which leads into the heart of the house.

The landing stage leads directly into François Spoerry's study, a vast, vaulted room filled with books on sailing, cars and the architectures of every country in the world. This room is decorated with quite superb models of the schooners and yachts which their owner commissioned, as much through his admiration for the craftsmen who executed them, as for his love of these magnificent objects.

It is here, to his study, that François Spoerry retires he wants to be alone to work, to think, to meditate. Here too, he receives visitors, his international partners, and more and more often, the succession of journalists, critics and writers interested in the history of Port Grimaud, the adventure that is Port Liberté, and the many projects which he is in the process of designing and building.

It is to this house that, with his wife Denise, he welcomes visitors and friends, though sadly he spends less time at home than he would wish. This is because his fame obliges him to fly to the four quarters of the globe to check on the progress of the various projects in hand. This considerable task is shared by his colleagues and top associates, among whom is his son Bernard, who, like his father, is an architect.

In order to remain in constant touch with his partners and the various developers, financiers and politicians with whom he works, François Spoerry has for years conducted an aerial ballet between Port Grimaud, Mulhouse, New York and Mexico. He visited both China and Indonesia in 1987 at the invitation of their governments, and in 1988 at the request of the Prime Minister and the Minister of Tourism, he visited Turkey where he was commissioned to undertake a major study of the protection of and usage of the principal sites for tourism both existing and potential along the length of Turkey's Mediterranean coast.

The subject of these investigative studies are often much closer to home, this, however, does not make them any less interesting. These commissions which most people would think challenging, suit François Spoerry's character, who long ago adopted Pascal's dictum "Life is motion" as his own. Life for Spoerry means a constant flow of ideas, of designs and projects with periods of fulsome enthusiasm, periods of frustrating set backs, he is neither discouraged nor bitter. He always has an unfailing fund of new ideas to replace those which may not have succeeded.

One suspects that such intense activity leaves François Spoerry little time to indulge his favourite past-times of sailing, organising extended sailing cruises in the company of friends, and navigation – for it was his passion for these three past-times that gave birth to his idea for Port Grimaud.

Claude Parent, the French architect, wrote of François Spoerry, that:

"He is the only French architect of international stature who has not allowed himself to become stereotyped. He has had the courage and the daring to take great risks, and at the head of his company he has blazes new trails in countries all over the world, an example that leading architects would do well to follow in the light of 1992. His work is poles apart from mine, and like so many others, I, at first, reserved judgement on Port Grimaud but I did not want to be either prejudiced or unfair, which is why having waited a long time, I eventually, and on two separate occasions, visited Port Grimaud and stayed quite some time. It really has the most wonderful atmosphere – it both works and is pleasing. It is not a little galling for contemporary architects who have been totally unable to create a similar pleasant and convivial atmosphere – despite their claims in their writings and lectures. François Spoerry really has thrown the architects of my generation into confusion."

If, as Claude Parent says, François Spoerry has come to be recognised as an architect of international stature, such recognition is due largely to the enormous success of Port Grimaud, and that, which is assured, of Port Liberté. However, it is also due in large measure to his attitude towards the public for whom he designs and builds.

It is not very often that contemporary architects, and especially the most ardent of the protagonists of the Modern Movement, live in houses or apartments which they themselves have designed and built. In the main, they prefer to live in old manor houses, ancient mills, magnificent houses, or simply the classic apartment – there are, of course, exceptions. François Spoerry, however, has chosen to live in the town he created. He and the shopkeepers around the Place du Marché were among the first to take up residence in Port Grimaud, a gesture which has earned Spoerry their admiration and sincere respect. They say:

"Our architect lives among us, and has never left, …we might have been his clients, we have become partners, and we hope, his friends. Whenever he returns from a trip, he always flies his flag from the top of his Saracen tower. We take this as a sign of friendship, really as if he is paying us a salute. And then too, we see him coming and going in his small boat up and down the canals between his office, his home and the building site of the final quarter of the town. Not only has he built houses which everyone likes, he has also created a little town with its many gardens, its trees and shrubs which flourish so splendidly. We really are most flattered that, unlike the architects who build blocks of council flats that they would never dream of living in, he lives among us."

Thus, in daily contact with his creation, his experience as a builder is constantly enriched and renewed.

"The only true barometer by which to measure the merits of an artist is the quality of the pleasure it provokes' wrote Stendhal in about 1830. This aphorism still holds good today and reflects the reaction of the public in its spontaneous and constant support of François Spoerry's *gentle architecture*, as well as their esteem for this most unpretentious and unaffected man, whose whole attitude and code of ethics adds up to his aesthetically pleasant and pleasing concept of life.

Marc Gaillard

François Spoerry at home
in Port Grimaud in 1988

It would be useless to seek the theorist in me. I am not at ease when faced with the reasoning of intellectuals and scientists. I prefer to look on myself more as a builder than an architect, in the manner of the architect-builders of the Renaissance.

My ambition has been to produce a style of architecture that makes the heart sing. An architecture that is quite the opposite of the stark, aggressive and mediocre architecture which was the norm when I started to practice my craft.

I dreamt only of *a gentle architecture.*

This XVIIth century print shows the village of Maennedorf, on Lake Zurich, birthplace of the Spœrry's since the end of the Middle Ages. At the extreme right of the picture are the family's three houses.

Towards a Gentle Architecture

A gentle architecture was revealed to me during my adolescence, when travelling with my father who, besides being passionately interested in dead languages, was also a brilliant Hellenist. I retain from those journeyings, a dazzling memory of discovering the Greek and Roman civilisations and their architecture, as well as that of local contemporary architecture, known today as vernacular architecture.

Four factors were to confirm my intuitive feelings about architecture, and were to contribute to the shaping of my development as an architect – my apprenticeship before going to the Beaux Arts; a study tour I made in Greece during my graduate year at the school; the teachings of my professor, Eugène Beaudoin; and my experiences in the Resistance and in the concentration camps.

In the thirties, candidates for the competitive entry examination to the Beaux Arts were expected to have a solid grounding in drawing. Accordingly, I spent a year as apprentice-draughtsman with Albert Doll, an architect in my birthplace, Mulhouse, before going on to become Jaques Couelle's assistant in 1932. At that time when very little building was taking place, Jaques Couelle, who is today a member of the Institute, ran a fascinating and complex business in which he managed to combine all the activities of an architect, interior decorator and antique dealer. Among other things he specialised in the restoration of medieval ruins and crumbling Spanish cloisters. The fragments he saved from these derelict buildings were promptly integrated in his own projects and developments in the South of France which gave them an indisputable air of authenticity.

He worked mostly on the Côte d'Azur and under his aegis I helped to build a number of attractive residences, such as the Bastide St-François at Grasse and Pigranel Castle which is between Castellaras and Mougins. The history of Pigranel is of particular interest. Having dismantled a small XVth century hunting-lodge at Is-sur-Tille in Burgundy we brought it to the South, where it was used as one of the *trompe l'œil* facades of a walled courtyard which, from the exterior, gave the impression of a fortress. The entrance was protected by a strongly built porch surmounted by a dovecote. The whole effect was intentionally theatrical. Years later, when I was about to tackle Port Grimaud, I remembered Pigranel.

Since then I have not had the opportunity of collaborating with Jaques Couelle and, much as I admire the projects he carried out at Castellaras and at Calla di Volpe in Sardinia, I was less enthusiastic about his Port-la-Galère. What is certain however is that the two years I worked with him were the finest imaginable initiation I could have had for my craft as a builder. The proof of this was that on leaving his employment I was placed first in the Beaux Arts examination of 1936 and immediately admitted to the Debat-Ponsan studio.

My first vocation was not architecture but the sea. So much so that I had prepared for the entrance examination to the Naval College in the special class at the Lycée St Louis in Paris. This is how, at the age of seventeen, I was lucky enough to make my first crossing to New York in the *Jaques Cartier*, the training ship for officer-cadets in the Merchant Navy.

But reality does not always measure up to one's dream. I soon became disenchanted with a career which appeared to consist mainly of routine work which I did not find in the least stimulating. So I was not too disappointed when I was obliged to abandon the Navy because of a minor problem with my eyesight. Although I was never commissioned I remained a sailor at heart. I am a *sailor-architect.*

While studying at the Beaux Arts I was haunted by a book I had read when I was twelve or thirteen years old.

Several generations of Spoerry's. Pictured above is great-grandfather, Henry Spoerry, who, from 1840, was responsible for the growth of the great textile industries of Mulhouse. Above right is Henry Spoerry, François Spoerry's father who instilled in his son his great love sailing and architecture. To the right is François Spoerry on board the training ship *Jacques Cartier* as it set sail for New York in 1929.

At the *Ecole des Beaux-Arts* at Strasbourg in 1930. The front row from right to left: René Schmitt, the future architect of *"Bâtiments de France"*, Robert Mayer, Jean Hatt and seated on the desk, François Spoerry.

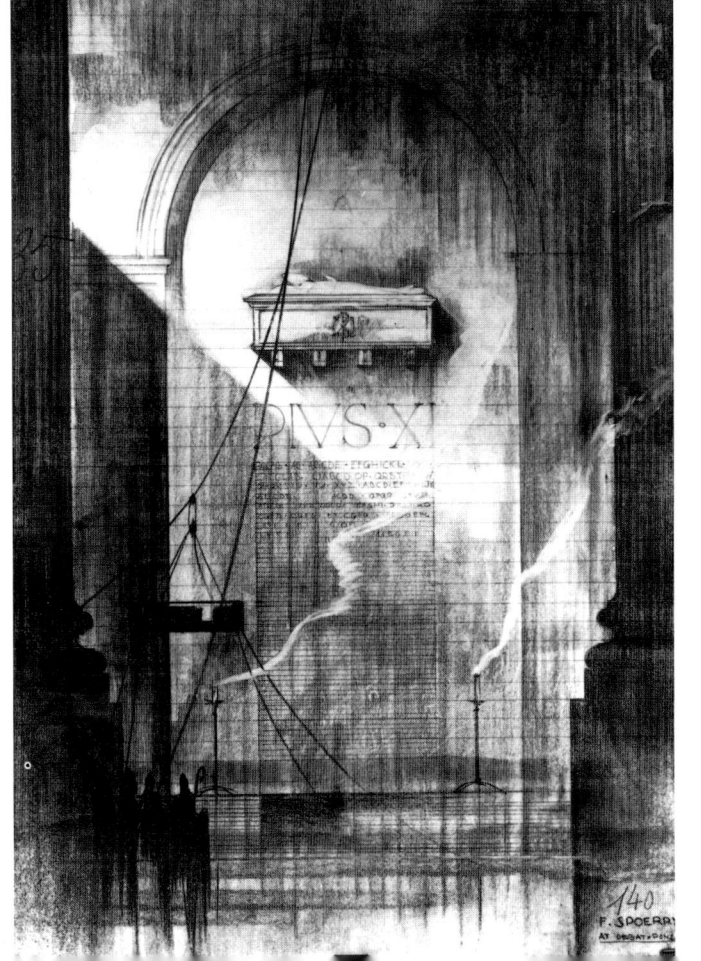

In 1929, François Spoerry designed part of his parents' holiday home at Cavalaire (above left). This commission marked the beginning of his career as an architect.
As the assistant to Jacques Couelle, he contributed to the rebuilding and restoration of Pigranel Castle, near Mougins, in which are incorporated elements of a Burgundian hunting lodge dating from the end of the XVth century (above right).

Design for the Tomb of a Pope. A project submitted for the first round of the *Prix de Rome* of 1937. The design had to be completed within twelve hours.

This was *The Cruise of the Perlette* which two archeologists, Hermine de Saussure and Marthe Ouillie had published in 1925. In it they wrote the story of their expedition and discoveries in the Aegean Sea. Going to Greece in those days bears no resemblance to the package tours of today. At that time the country was shaken by political undercurrents and was virtually unknown to tourists. In as much as this tale whetted my appetite for adventure the book by these two women seemed to invite me to explore a great unknown heritage. I longed to follow in their footsteps. I managed to convince the Minister of National Education, Jean Zay, to give me an assignment in Greece. My mission was to make an inventory of all the principal features and characteristics of vernacular architecture. I sold my car and bought a 10.5 metre yacht and, throughout the winter helped by four of my friends from the Beaux Arts, I equipped, tried and tested my craft at Cavalaire where my family had a house. In the spring of 1939 the sturdy little *Colibri* set sail.

How can I ever forget our Odyssey at a time when Europe and the Mediterranean were in a state of turmoil? The Italian ports of call made a tremendous impression on us. From Messina we sailed to Patras but we could not get through the Corinth Canal as it had been damaged by an earthquake. So we skirted the Peloponnese as far as

The design for the restoration of a washhouse that led to his being placed first in the 1936 entrance examinations to the *Ecole des Beaux-Arts* in Paris.

Athens using a makeshift chart no bigger than the palm of my hand. To our great surprise we found the *Perlette* anchored a few cable lengths from our *Colibri*. Though it was past eleven at night I jumped into my dinghy and tacking into the port was able, at long last, to gaze at the mythical ship that had determined my career.

How can I explain the euphoria that gripped us when we relaxed in the Cyclades, exploring and sketching in the menacing shadow of the war that was now imminent?

Nor shall I ever forget the volcanic eruption which woke us the night we were anchored off the Island of Santorini. Having immediately weighed anchor, we were able to admire the awesome spectacle of the great jets of smoke and gas belching out of the mountain and into the seething, bubbling waters of the bay. At Santorini we heard that hostilities had started and mobilisation begun. So, in order to hasten our journey to our units, we abandoned our trip in the *Colibri* together with all our documentation and reports and entrusted her to Greek friends who undertook to sail her back to Athens.

Unfortunately they were shipwrecked and the *Colibri* sank with all hands as well as all our precious notes and papers. But, although little remained of our sketches, this assignment had enabled me both to discover the perfection and simplicity of vernacular architecture and to make a careful in-depth study of the general layout of the dwellings. In addition I observed closely a multiplicity of details including stairs, cupolas, the positioning of windows and air vents, and the way in which the alleyways had been designed and built so as to offer maximum protection both from the sun and from the *Melten*, the prevailing wind that blows so violently in the Cyclades.

I was never to forget the many ports of call at which we touched on the voyage and the many stimulating discoveries we made which provoked such intense emotional reaction in us. All these were clear and fresh in my memory when I began my own life as a builder.

As soon as I got back to France I went to the Barracks at Angers where I was put in charge of recruits to whom I taught the rudiments of pioneer engineering. After a few months in Versailles during which I received my commission, I was sent to the Somme and, having seen both fighting and retreat, I made my way south where I enrolled myself in Eugène Baudouin's studio in Marseilles where he had taken refuge during the Occupation.

Eugène Baudouin was one of the finest professors at the National School of the Beaux-Arts. His liberal teaching methods were not influenced by the theories of functionalism although he and Marcel Lods were its chief defenders. He was the classic example of a man of absolute integrity who supported and advocated contemporary architecture fairly and honestly, without

Sketches drawn in the Cyclades in 1939.
These mark the discovery of a *Gentle Architecture* born out of the spontaneous fusion of the climate and the local life-style.

sectarianism. He was a cultured man who, unlike others, was prepared to admit that architectural projects could be approached in many different ways. Baudouin had a stout heart and was a loyal and faithful friend. While working with him I prepared for my diploma which I received in 1942. The theme I chose for my examination was "A Naval Dockyard". At the same time I collaborated with my friends, Jean Hatt and Pierre Martin, in compiling a book on traditional Provençal architecture for which I did the local research. This followed my meeting with Professor Jean Bernard who was responsible for running several resistance groups in the South of France. Later I was to learn that Buckmaster's networks formed the active French section of the Intelligence Service whose director was a mysterious "Dick" (this alias concealed the real identity of Richard Badington, British writer and journalist). Maurice Druon and Joseph Kessel, both famous writers, and the great singer Germaine Sablon belonged to this network into which I was later introduced. It was known as the Jean-Marie and, like so many of the others, was organised and run by Jean Bernard. Our work consisted of locating safe landing zones for planes and parachutists and liaising with the pilots of the Lysanders – those small silent British aircraft which were reputed to be able to land and turn on a sixpence and which carried enough fuel to fly from England to Provence and back. Another aspect of our work was concerned with collecting information about German units stationed in Provence and particularly in Toulon. In Paris, my sister Anne Spoerry ran a safe house and was responsible for taking in and looking after British parachutists who landed in the Occupied Zone, and for making arrangements to get them through to the Free Zone. A family property lying off the beaten track in the commune of Rognes near Aix-en-Provence was the headquarters of our radio operations. Sadly one of our companions was arrested by the Gestapo and "turned". He obtained his freedom by pretending to escape having named names. On the 17th of April I was arrested at Aix. A few days later the Germans pounced on my sister in Paris. I had recently bought a lovely old house, known as l'hotel d'Espagnet, one of the few private houses on the Cours Mirabeau in Aix-en-Provence. It was used as a hideout and weapons belonging to the members of our network were stashed away in false rafters. Despite a thorough search they were not found but I was marched off to the old and sinister prison Saint Pierre de Marseilles. I was then transferred to Fresnes where I was interrogated and detained in one of the death cells. My sister was deported to Ravensbruck and eventually I was moved to Neue-Bremme near Sarrebrücken where I witnessed the death of Colonel Daum, a member of the famous family of master-glassworkers of Lorraine. I was then sent to Buchenwald; then to Dora, a natural grotto in the Hardt Mountains, where we dug tunnels intended to transform the site into a vast arsenal to house V2 rockets. From there I was transferred to Struthoff and then to Erzingen, near Lake Constance, before finally moving to Dachau where I learned that the Allies had landed in Normandy and later, in Provence. I was freed in May 1945.

My experience in the concentration camps, like those of so many others, showed me the true dimensions of the human condition in both its greatness and its misery. This also helped me to change my personal opinions and to make different evaluations. Aged thirty I was not too old to suffer terribly from being ill-treated and deprived of liberty, nor was I young enough to commit the folly of trying to escape as so many of my companions had done. Inevitably they were brought back and shot. First at Fresnes and then in the other camps I learned that to survive I had to preserve my strength. I forced myself to forget the horror of my present situation and to think only of the future. With makeshift drawing materials I tried to sustain my companions by sketching the houses of their dreams, the homes in which they would live as free men after the war. For hours we discussed ways of making the facade of a house impervious to the ocean gales and where exactly to place picture windows so as to frame the best views, as well as planning every room in each particular houses we were designing.

Deportation made me differentiate clearly and forever between matters that are essential and those of secondary importance. It also taught me to distinguish between events arising in one's own life which were important and those which were less so. Looking back, I now realise that it is a combination of all these factors which enabled me to conceive of a *Gentle Architecture*.

In point of fact I did not originate the term *Gentle Architecture*. To the best of my knowledge it appeared in an issue of *Architecture d'aujourd'hui* in May 1975. The editors of the journal used the words in a different, more craft-orientated and environmentally-conscious context. At the same time they readily admitted that *Gentle Architecture* could take on many forms and variations. So far as I am concerned I feel more in sympathy with the definition they used which is opposed to any form of artificial, monumental or institutional type of architecture.

However at the very time that I was establishing my own architectural practice surrounded by colleagues who, like myself, admired traditional village architecture and all that was built in the time honoured style, a new master of architecture with a persuasive tongue and who brooked no argument as to his teachings, was becoming known internationally. His name was Le Corbusier. I was destined to suffer cruelly, both intellectually and physically, from the infatuation of my contemporaries with his style of *modern architecture*. Even if I did not have to endure his tyranny, his work dominated the entire architectural scene from 1950 inspiring all architects and serving as the only point of reference for the critics.

Myths of Modern Architecture

If Le Corbusier's vision was innovative his influence was even more harmful than it seemed. This was because it was backed by exceptional talent which enabled him to put forward absurd theories which were to take in millions of people and make them unhappy.

In 1929 Le Corbusier wrote an article in the newspaper *L'Intransigeant* in which he set the scene for the bombshell he was about to launch on an unsuspecting public...

A road, pavements, walls, houses whose silhouette tear great gaps in the sky. The street is on the slum in which this adventure takes place. It is bathed in eternal shadow; far, far, above, the blue sky offers only faint and distant hope. The street is a channel, a deep fissure, a narrow corridor. One can span this corridor between two heart-beats! ...The street is made of a thousand different dwellings. Their proximity creates a hideous cacophony of sound, it is ghastly ...It is the street of the pedestrian of the millennium, a left-over of the centuries, a useless limb without any proper function. The street uses us, shaming and creating disorder in our towns ...

We are disgusted. Why is such a street allowed to remain? ...Logic and reason provide us with dazzling solutions! ...which lead us towards a new social contract.

Le Corbusier painted an idyllic picture of a new social contract incorporating a new kind of town planning:

You will live under trees, surrounded by limitless expanses of green lawns. The air will be pure and there will be scarcely any noise. ...At a great distance one from the other, will be gigantic glass shapes sparkling in the sky and seeming to float in

Some sad examples of 'brutalist' architecture: arid, repetitive and with total disregard for the site, these *'machines for living'* are the product of a wholly functional approach to design.

the air rather than to touch the earth. ...Thanks to the magical properties of electricity these shapes will twinkle in the night. The roof gardens of the buildings appear to be golden bridges flung across the night from which one may discern the distant roar which comes from the ancient, time-encrusted districts of Paris. ...A new blueprint for building will appear to replace the state of misery into which the white races have allowed themselves to be engulfed.

This vision of the future owes as much to science-fiction as to Jean-Jaques Rousseau's ideology. Once put into practice, it proved an enormous hoax. Far from producing glittering glass set amidst verdant landscapes, it gave rise to a rash of high rise blocks in an outbreak of leprosy which affected our entire urban civilisation.

But Le Corbusier was a great and honey-tongued communicator. He knew exactly the right words and formulas to get his message across. This, combined with the fervent zeal of the convert, served to convince the majority of architects of my generation.

The *Radiant City* bears the hallmark of forceful lyricism interspersed with semi-magical phrases which so seduced his contemporaries that none of them dared question or infringe his precepts which rapidly became dogma.

The aim of the International Congress for Modern Architecture, held in 1933, was supposedly to find contemporary solutions to the problems of architecture and housing. The Congress stood squarely behind Le Corbusier's theories and, under his leadership, published the famous *Athens Charter* which became as famous a reference book as the Bible.

Le Corbusier's influence was doubly dangerous for the transformations he advocated needed the backing of knowledge and techniques that were lacking at this particular time. The urgent needs of communities, whose towns and villages had been ravaged by war, the ever increasing number of people and the lack of expertise or mastery of modern techniques, all condemned these grandiose concepts to certain failure.

But Le Corbusier's statements fell upon receptive ears and the seeds he sowed fell on fertile ground thus encouraging their growth. The battle cry was Modernisation at any price. The teachings of the Beaux Arts were reviled as "tattered academic rags". This sorry state of

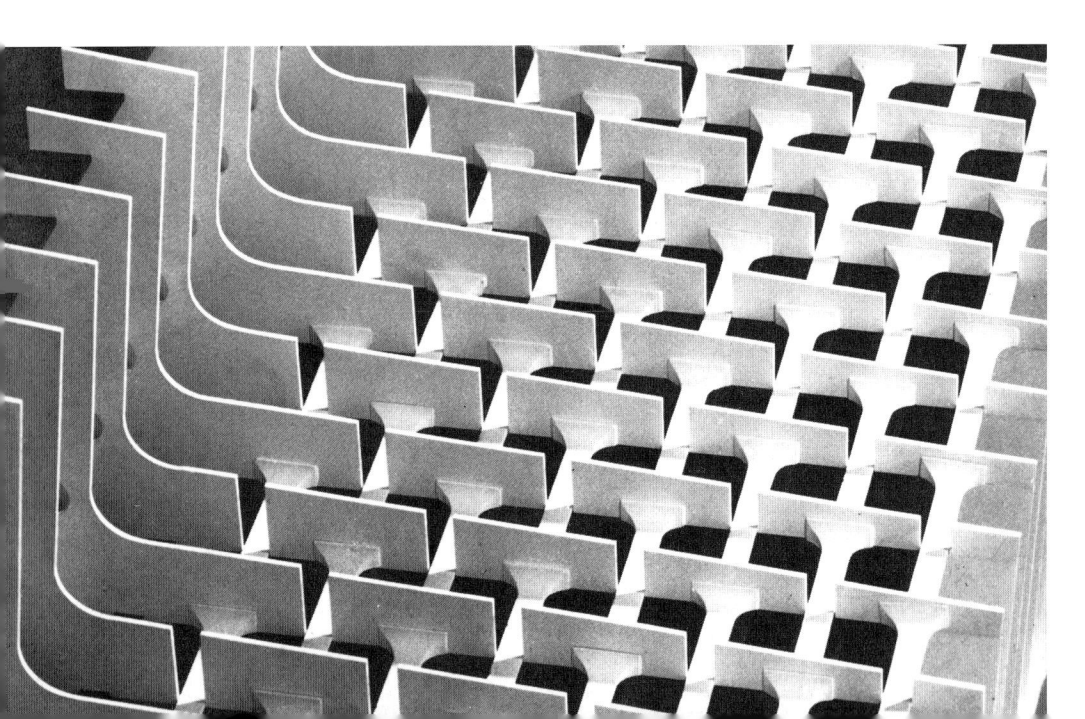

Millions of individuals used as guinea-pigs... But where are the *"crystal tower-blocks of the Radiant City"* of which Le Corbusier spoke?

affairs was not limited to France. It was an international phenomenon manifest throughout the world by the total rejection of all past architectural work to the new academicism. Did not Walter Gropius on becoming Dean of Architecture at Harvard University banish all work consecrated to the traditional architecture of the past from the bookshelves of the the Fine Arts Library? In order to be *modern* it was deemed essential to break with all trace of traditions and with the millenary techniques used in building. Nor must any reference be made to traditional cultures. The art historian Charles Jencks emphasises how ably the intellectual and abstract characteristics of modern architecture were propped up by untested axioms, supposedly related to the needs of man. These vacuous theories existed only in the heads of the architects, who grew ever more remote from the requirements of real people. He noted that the exaggeratedly quantitative and analytical approach to the housing problem led to divorce between those who conceived these ideas and those forced to accept and live with them. Is not talking about "a machine to live in" tantamount to comparing a home to a consumer product created by a technical society?

The words "apartments" or "houses" were banished in favour of "cells". Functional architecture and scientific town-planning may have led to an increase in space and comfort, but the unprecedented growth of repetitive schemes for schools and offices, with their total lack of any kind of decorative or artistic detail, or ornament, produced a feeling of complete sterility. The triumph of modern architecture was to advocate a clean sweep of all that had once made it great, allied to a vandalism which was sufficiently pretentious to try and replace an inheritance of immeasurable quality, crafted down to the minutest detail, by massive tower blocks. More building took place in thirty years than in the previous twenty centuries; accumulations of concrete erections identical in their mediocrity and distressingly banal.

"The decadence of civilisation can be put down to the degeneration of the home", wrote Le Corbusier, who was second to none in his use of language, as well as considering himself something of a visionary. The real reasons for the decadence of architecture were attributable to ideology and intellectualism.

Modern architecture was complemented by the theory and practice of modern town planning. In furthering their chosen ideology the developers indulged in abstract experiments which involved millions of people being used as guinea-pigs, and all in the name of science. Purely technical experiments suddenly replaced the slow and continuous biological formation and growth which so characterised towns and villages formerly. I heartily endorse the sentiments expressed by Paolo Portoghesi in his work *Beyond Modern Architecture*...

A small group of people from fast-developing countries put forward the claim that it was possible to establish a universal language and a set of universal rules for practical architecture. Never has any such scheme put into practice by a minority that had so strong and such far-flung an influence without physical or cultural limitations. ...Thus did the planet become a hopeless prison. ...Town planning was replaced by "zoning" or, to put it another way, by codifying a city into orderly ghettos supposedly built with the aim of helping mankind to achieve a better

life-style. The truth was that these theories about "zoning", which were both inexplicable and corrupt, sounded the death-knell of modern civilisation.

More astonishing still was the fact that the very authorities supposedly responsible for the economic and political framework of social and communal life seemed to be totally devoid of any critical faculties. Between July 1971 and December 1974, a weekly series of television programmes entitled *"la France défigurée"* was shown nation-wide. It did not, however, attack the two main factors responsible for the mutilation of the countryside: the so-called modern town planning, and modern architecture. By this was meant the crazy proliferation of houses in squalid and anarchic settings. Most of the sites chosen lacked any kind of cohesion and all this was happening at the very moment of "the great leap forward" in the building industry. The effect of all of this was to wipe out our heritage both in towns and in the countryside. And this architectural cacophony was orchestrated by town councillors, property developers representing both municipal and private companies as well as communities, and the media. The only problems journalists were willing to discuss were those concerned with bath taps! They never protested against failures or architectural standards; they protested strongly against any lack of technology and were delighted when they managed to give their readers the impression that all architects and developers were dangerous villains.

Furthermore none of the specialist architectural and building magazines ever analysed the reasons for the decline of academic principles, or why aesthetic and emotional values had been replaced by purely intellectual and abstract ideas. So, in the space of thirty years, in support of these theories, harmony was destroyed, the balance of our cities upset, our countryside ruined and all the old scales modified. The modern city built on the principle of "zoning" is artificial and unattractive. It causes stress and tension for those who live there. Dual-carriageways and motorways have carved up space, abolished neighbourly relationships, complicated travel and isolated certain suburbs in such a way as to make them almost inaccessible.

Gigantic high-rise tower blocks proliferate and threaten the skyline with their brutal and aggressive bulk. Vital living space has been used with no recourse to reason or logic. The result was that neither the eye nor the spirit could find rest, calm or contentment in the concrete jungles. The cosy, friendly muddles of the past were exchanged for soulless, built vulgarity.

Having made the error of confusing residents with citizens and passive acceptance with sharing, town planners and architects have managed to alienate the general public who, in any case, were not involved in their academic and doctrinal squabbles. I maintain that the individual must not be thought of only as a client, but as a partner. Neither should one sneer at the people, nor at the great traditions on which our civilisation has been built.

My first step was to rebel against the intellectual tyranny and the doctrines held by contemporary architects, and to try to compensate for their blindness by thinking how a new renaissance could be brought about.

The Art of Living

When I opened my own office I could not wait to reject the uniformity which then prevailed.

My beginnings in Mulhouse, in a France so devastated by the Second World War, were modest. I began by carrying out a series of small jobs repairing essential war-damage, as listed in the official files. But owing to the constant harassment and caprices of the local Administration this was a pretty thankless task, although it did allow me to discover the building restrictions currently in force. There was a complete lack of materials and equipment; every single bag of cement, every metre of steel reinforcement for concrete had to be accounted for.

Eventually, I was given more interesting and taxing projects such as the re-building of the elegant neo-classical head office of the *Société Industrielle* standing in one of Mulhouse's most enchanting squares and built during the period of the First Empire. Another rewarding contract was for the restoration of the fine building housing the Chamber of Commerce. Twenty years later, Emile Muller, the Mayor of Mulhouse, entrusted me with the responsibility of the design and town planning of an area of seven hectares, the former site of textiles factories. It was here that I created the Place de l'Europe. Above the main bus station I built a square surrounded by a variety of shops and commercial enterprises. I thought it might be

By the 1950s, Spoerry affirms his dedication to the concept of "the art of building for the art of living", whether in the countryside, as with this comfortable house near Mulhouse; or in the town, with a square, the Place de l'Europe at Mulhouse, in which a terminus for various means of transport is combined with a centre of activities.

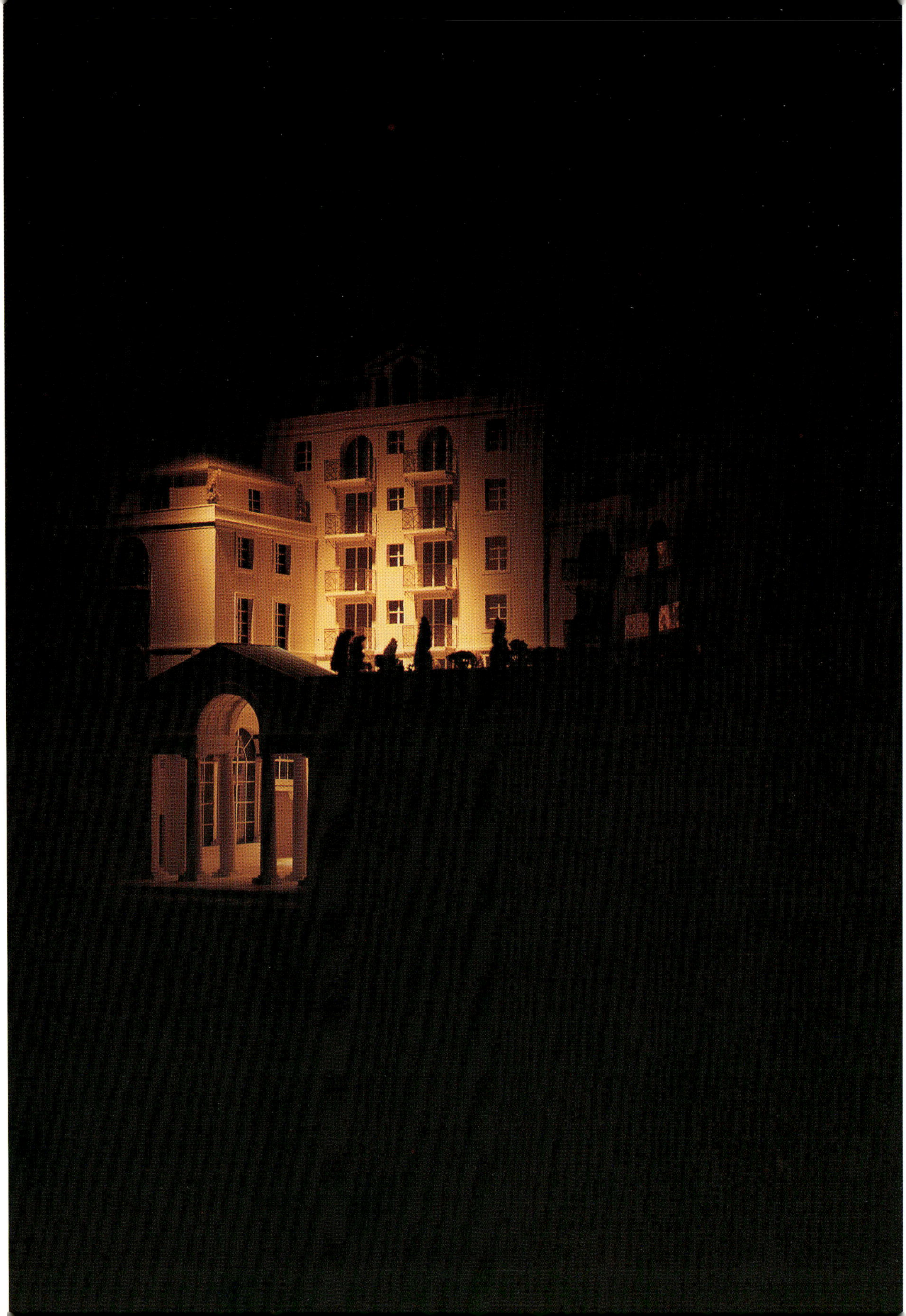

interesting to endow this flat and somewhat uninteresting region, on the Plain of Alsace, with a symbol in the form of a kind of tower or belfry. The main feature of the structure was a triangular tower in the shape of a three-pointed star (rectangular structures being then the fashion) which was a hundred and ten metres high. This was the Tour de l'Europe which today towers above the city and can be seen for miles around. At the very top I installed a revolving restaurant. Each rotation lasted approximately the time taken to finish a meal. The very mild speed of rotation stopped the customers from feeling giddy! and let them enjoy a panorama of the surrounding countryside. Although I did not invent this system, which was already in use in similar establishments abroad – particularly in Germany – I was the first to introduce it to France.

I could not really put my theories and ideas into practice until I built apartment blocks and residential suburbs of which I was both master-designer and master-builder. In Mulhouse, I built two thousand five hundred flats in the districts of Pierrefontaine and Entremont. I tried to break away from the standards generally associated with building large apartment blocks by concentrating on my concept of town planning and the siting of buildings. Above all, I wanted to avoid gigantic tower blocks and to relate the size of my buildings to their surroundings. I think I can justifiably claim that my work stood out from the stereotyped buildings erected at the same time. I tried to treat my projects rather in the style of the pre-war garden cities and to create an acceptable form of architecture displaying none of the features which are mere sacrifices to fashion. I wanted to create an impression of dignity. What was also of the utmost importance to me was that whatever I created should be of high quality and appeal to the purchaser. These principles should surely be among an architect's foremost preoccupations. It is vitally important to pay particular attention to the setting or "framework" in which life is lived. Jaques Rigaud wrote some very lucidly on this very subject:

Whether monumental, familiar or practical, or whether they relate to a festival or to a dream, surroundings are a collection of signs, the mirror of a society which reflects the image of each personage of which it is composed. Thus they express some very profound truths.

If the criteria of cost and profitability are deemed to be of greater importance than considerations of quality or of happiness, or if the latter are allowed to play a purely decorative and subsidiary part, culture is forever compromised in the mind of man, and one should not be surprised, therefore, at his lack of concern or interest in such matters. If, on the contrary, society is prepared to subordinate material things in favour of life in a framework of quality, the path of cultural progess remains open since culture is recognised in its proper connotation as "city rights".

Recently completed at Mulhouse are two major undertakings which go to prove the architect's continuing search for both the quality of usage and a respect for the environment. They are, to the left, the Résidence Charles X (completed in 1989) which comprises both housing and offices, and to the right, the Entremont residential complex (which was built in the 1970s).

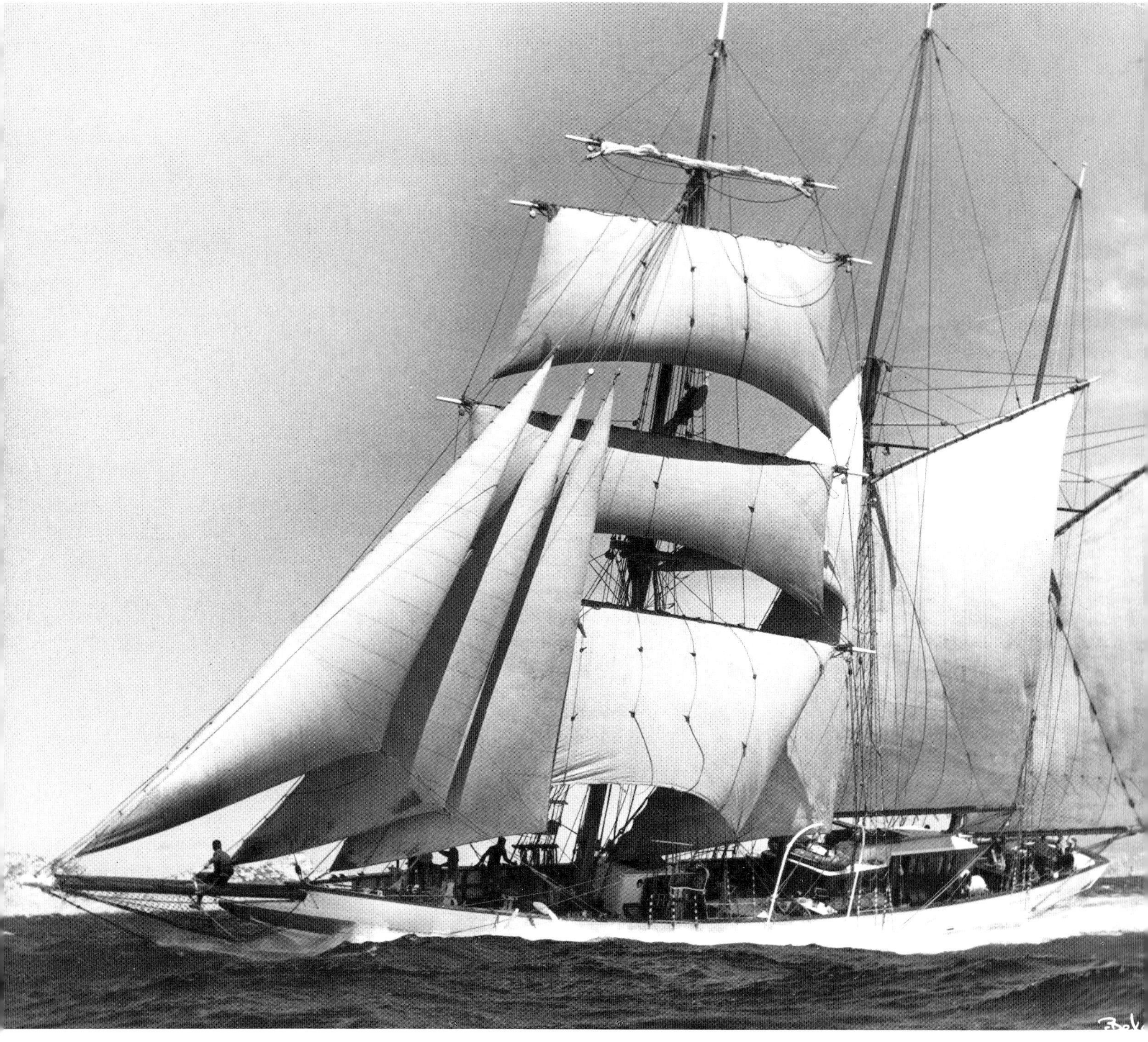

A Swamp in the Bay of St Tropez

The planning and construction of Port Grimaud enabled me not only to fulfil my dreams and hopes in concrete form, but also gave me the opportunity to give expression to my concept of architecture. Having acquired a site I was able to work unhindered and without being responsible to anyone but myself. I was, at the same time, developer, designer and master-builder – a situation which broke with all the accepted rules, and this was at a time when the architectural establishment looked upon a freelance as no better than a heretic. The stand I took caused a tremendous outcry in the profession.

My team and I certainly departed from the usual rules but the originality of our ideas allowed us to introduce aesthetic and technical qualities which would have been impossible had we been obliged to follow the normal procedures. This involved the division of decisions and responsibilities which inevitably arise in the planning and creation of a scheme. However, these do not, in themselves, guarantee success. I see nothing incompatible with being both property developer and master-builder; the two professions are complementary. The organisation and planning of the work are the responsibility of the foreman, its conception that of the master-builder. Down the centuries many architects have combined the work of both designer and developer at the same time. The artificial barriers between architectural design, which is in essence an abstraction, and the construction of that design which is very tangible, must

Port Grimaud was born out of both a passion for sailing ships and a love of the sea. Spoerry is to be seen here at the helm of his schooner, the *Amphitrite* and taking an active part in promoting his new project, as he ploughs through the waters of the Mediterranean.

Above left, an aerial view of the mouth of the Giscle in the Bay of St Tropez in 1965 – this was to become the site of Port Grimaud.

Left, a model of the first study of Port Grimaud, the design was the subject of a number of modifications before it was finally executed.

To the left, a study for the Grand Canal at Port Grimaud, 1965.
To the right, Port Grimaud as seen from the air, with at its centre, its church, its town-hall and Market Square. From this focal point radiates the many peninsulas, each bordered by houses "their feet in the water", and their boats at their moorings.

not be erected; nor between these two and the ability to finance a project.

This is why, before embarking on my new project, I formed a company with various subdivisions, one of which guaranteed the financing of any property deal for which I was the architect.

I have already mentioned that the Côte d'Azur, from the region of the Maures to that of Esterel, was familiar territory to me. Before the war I had often stayed and worked in those parts.

I have also alluded to my passion for the sea and for boats. I was heartily tired of having to use improvised moorings which always gave one a sense of insecurity since every puff of wind might seriously damage one's yacht. I was bored too with having to get up in the middle of the night to fend off the ravages of the *mistral*.

From time immemorial sailors have always wanted to keep their boats under close supervision moored in a calm water. Even as a child, I remember being fascinated by the models of prehistoric lagoon towns which were displayed at the Landesmuseum in Zurich. I longed to live in a modern version of these lakeside settlements. I had given up all hope of finding a suitable but available creek for the project of my dreams on the Côte d'Azur

finally convincing myself that a flat site on the water's edge might be the answer. It was simply a case of finding enough building land between the coast road and the sea – for a yacht cannot use a bridge. Eventually I came to the conclusion that the layout of the land at the far end of the Bay of St Tropez might be suitable, in spite of its swamps and sandbanks.

Thirty-five hectares were for sale but buyers were not interested. Presumably they were nervous of tackling what appeared to be an inhospitable, mosquito-ridden swamp. At first sight it seemed to be one of the least attractive places on the whole coast. I realised that the only way to make it remotely attractive was to visualise the sort of town that might be built on this unpromising site. For is it not the role of the architect to imagine what enchantment he can coax from what appears to be only waste ground?

Permission to build at Port Grimaud was first sought in 1963. Three years later, after overcoming innumerable objections and pitched battles with the various government bodies concerned, a permit was granted on the 14th of June 1966 and Port Grimaud, like Venus, can be said "to have risen from the waves". The birth of Port Grimaud, an historic event, was celebrated by the christening one of the first squares of the embryonic town, the Place du 14 Juin.

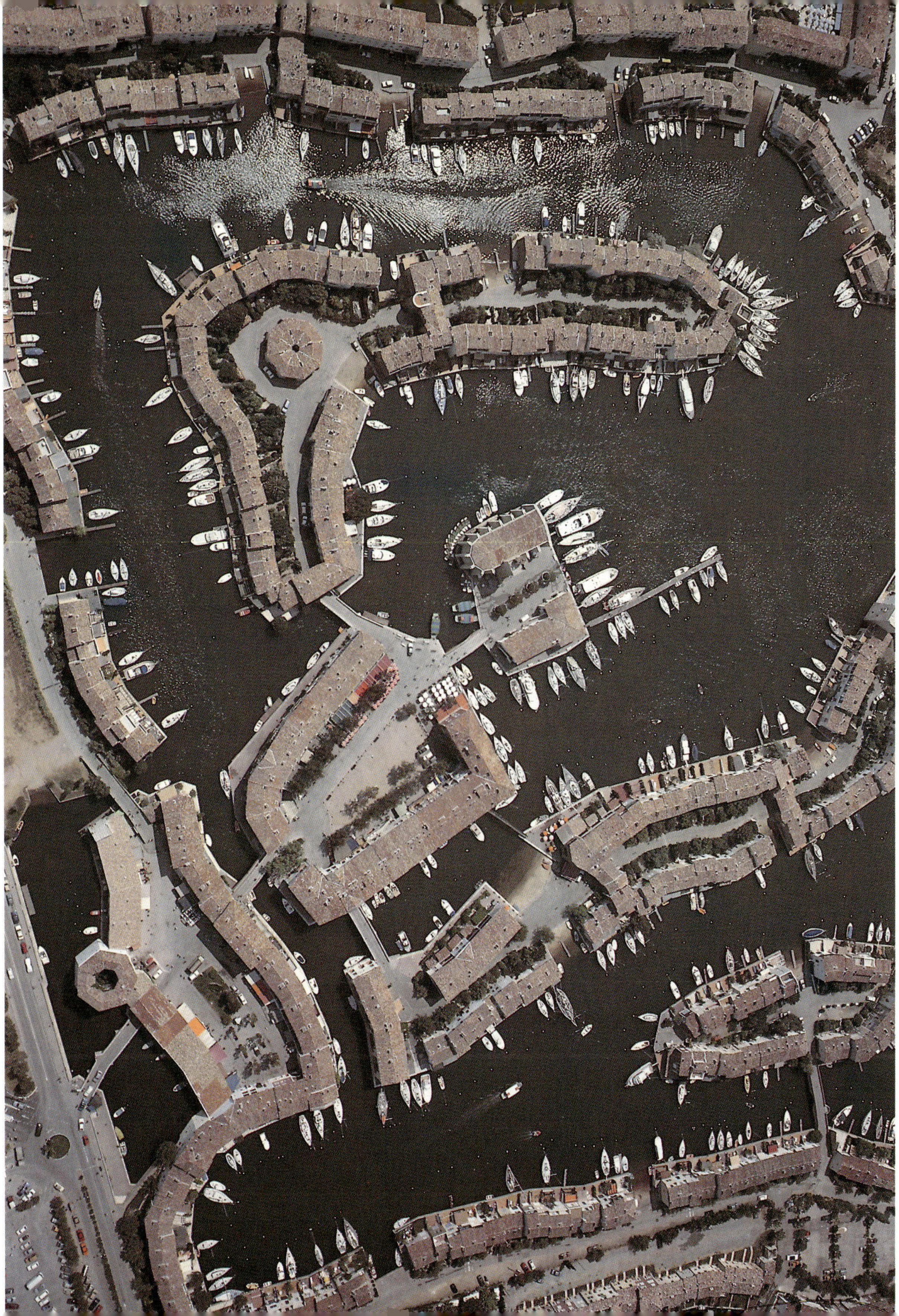

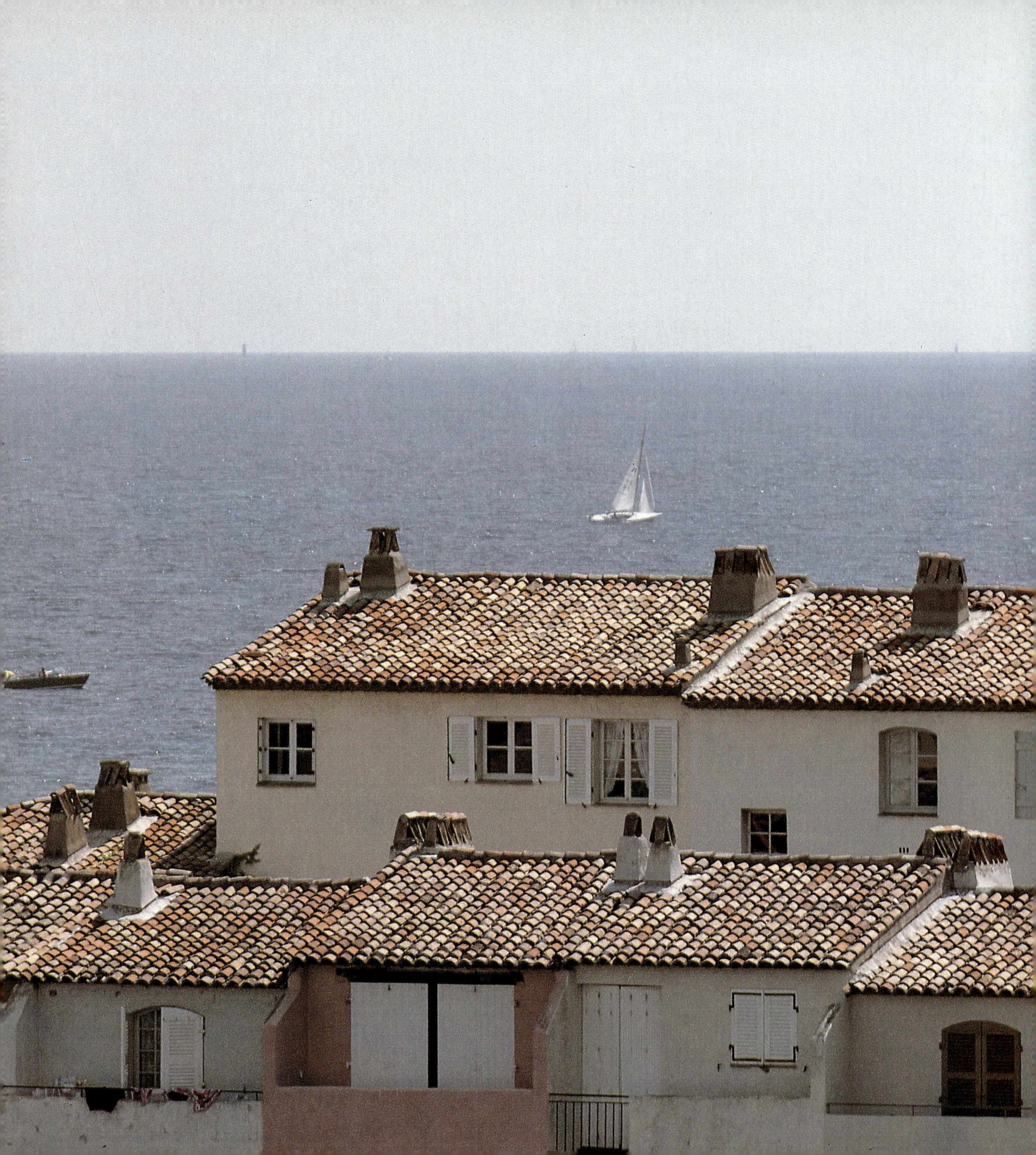

The peace and simplicity of *Gentle Architecture*.

All that now remained was to find the necessary finance to start building. The contacts I approached made it abundantly clear that they considered my project doomed to failure and refused to invest in it. I managed to get a bank loan of three million francs, a meagre and ridiculous sum compared with the magnitude of the task ahead.

It was therefore decided that if we wanted to go ahead quickly we should have to proceed piecemeal, completing each section, making it habitable as swiftly as possible, so that the sale of the houses in one section would guarantee the cash flow for the next, as well as offering a pleasant life-style to the owners of the first houses.

The initial photographs of Port Grimaud showing the new houses with their owner's yachts moored at quays at the end of each garden, made a tremendous impact on the general public, though my team and I were subjected to a stream of corny jokes and general hilarity all round. Some wags maintained that we had transported the yachts on lorries to the first canal when it was not connected to the sea! None of which prevented Port Grimaud from becoming a great commercial success. The resale value of the first houses rocketed while the prices of subsequent houses were kept in line with current market prices.

The enormous success of Port Grimaud was not just a flash in the pan, though it certainly did not lack critics who tried to ridicule me for building bridges over solid ground which I later turned into canals. These canals were specifically designed to enable yachts be moored astern to their own jetties. The 4 metre foundations on which the houses were built were specifically designed to correspond with the jetties. Only yachts of much greater tonnages were obliged to moor at the public quay.

The seven kilometres of canals which wind through the town provide the setting for a most intimate union of houses and boats; even when glimpsing over roof-tops with their Roman tiles the marine landscape is ever present.

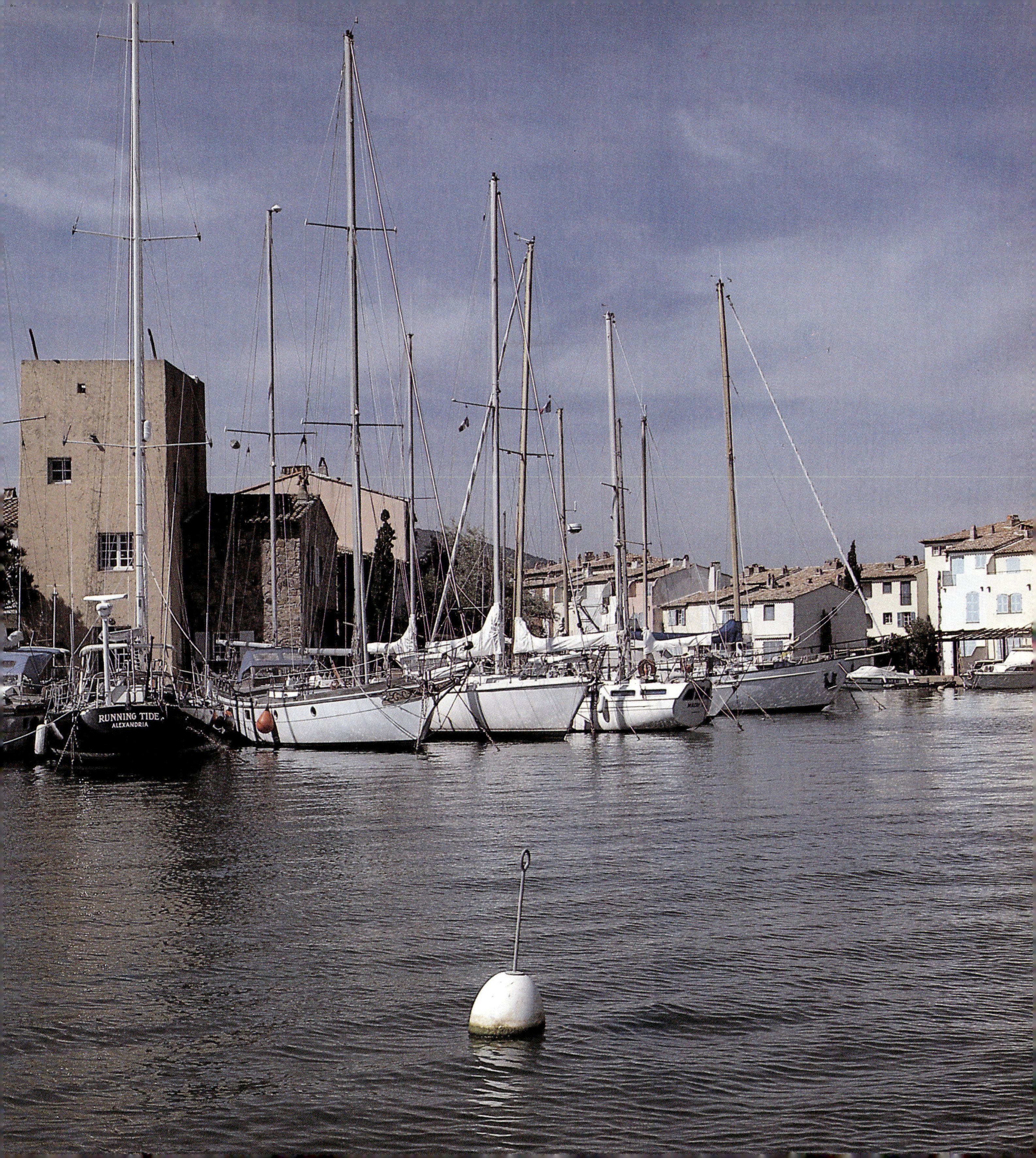
RUNNING TIDE
ALEXANDRIA

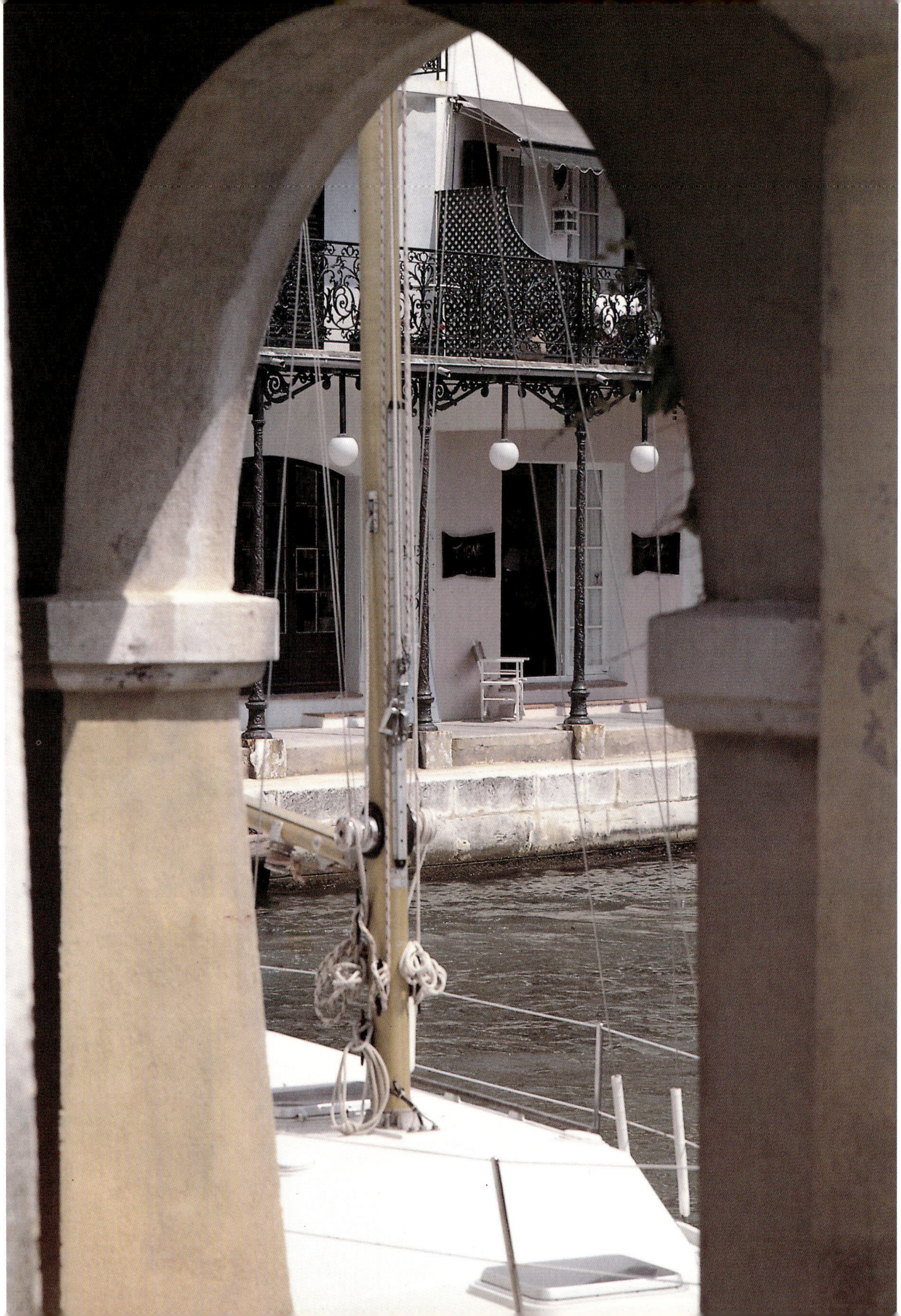

Their presence in the centre of the town, near the Church and Town Hall and facing the main square, contributed to the nautical atmosphere and poetic ambience which I had wanted to bring to my creation and which appeals to every sailor's heart. A key factor in the planning was my determination to banish cars from the interior of the town. As it was reasonable to suppose that its residents would be mainly interested in nautical pursuits we decided to give them the means of getting around, unimpeded by cars, on the canals in motor launches or in rowing boats. From the beginning my team and I decided that each house should have a good view over the water. There were to be no privileged exceptions. That is why on the original plans, peninsulas and canals were linked like the fingers on both hands.

Building a lagoon town behind a natural shoreline was an entirely new concept. Purely from a town-planning angle, this enabled us to increase the sea frontage, thereby lessening the speculative pressures on the coast

Differences in volume, the individual choice of the colour of each facade with respect to those of its neighbours, the colours being assigned from a palette of fourteen colours, and the most meticulous attention to the smallest detail explain why twenty years were needed to build the town.

itself and thereby avoiding very high density building near the shore. By increasing the possibilities of direct access to the sea we added an extra 14 kilometres to the French coast.

These factors seemed to impress foreign governments several of whom subsequently invited me to submit plans for similar projects. In France, however, our experience was not viewed sympathetically and the erosion of the coast continued unabated.

In Port Grimaud, whether one looks landwards or out to sea, one's gaze automatically falls upon the tall masts of sailing boats.

Port Grimaud even became the target of the most virulent criticism from within the architectural profession itself, on the grounds that what we had created did not conform to the style of architecture then in fashion. Plainly, *Gentle Architecture* was not acceptable.

There were times when I wondered whether anyone at all in the world of architecture shared my views or had the slightest understanding of what had prompted me to build Port Grimaud. A letter, that arrived quite out of the blue, broke through the fog like a beam from a lighthouse. It was from that grand old architect Clough Williams Ellis, creator of Portmeirion and many other successful schemes. Congratulating me on Port Grimaud, he added that he was happy to find an architect-builder who, like himself, also believed in traditional architecture.

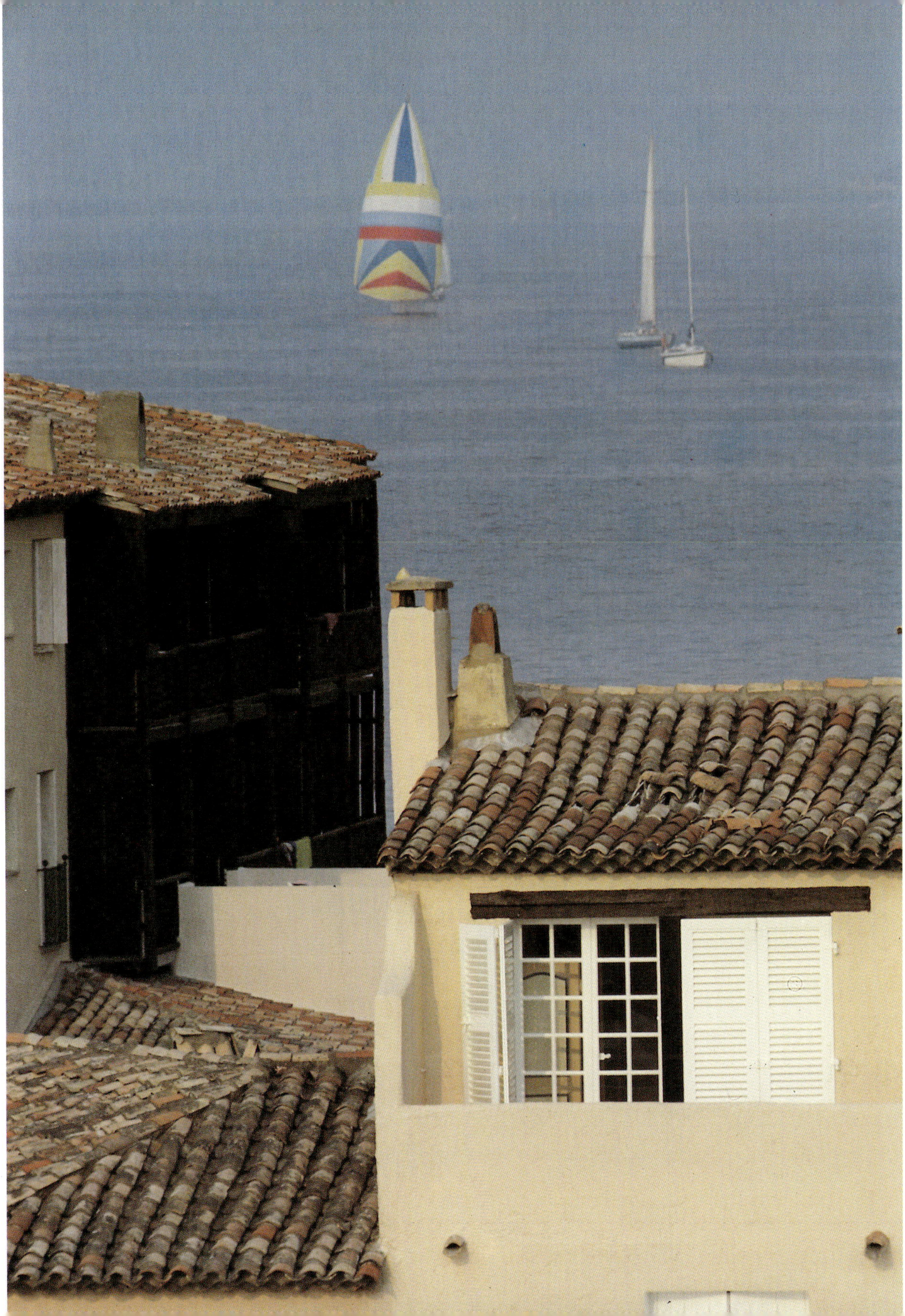

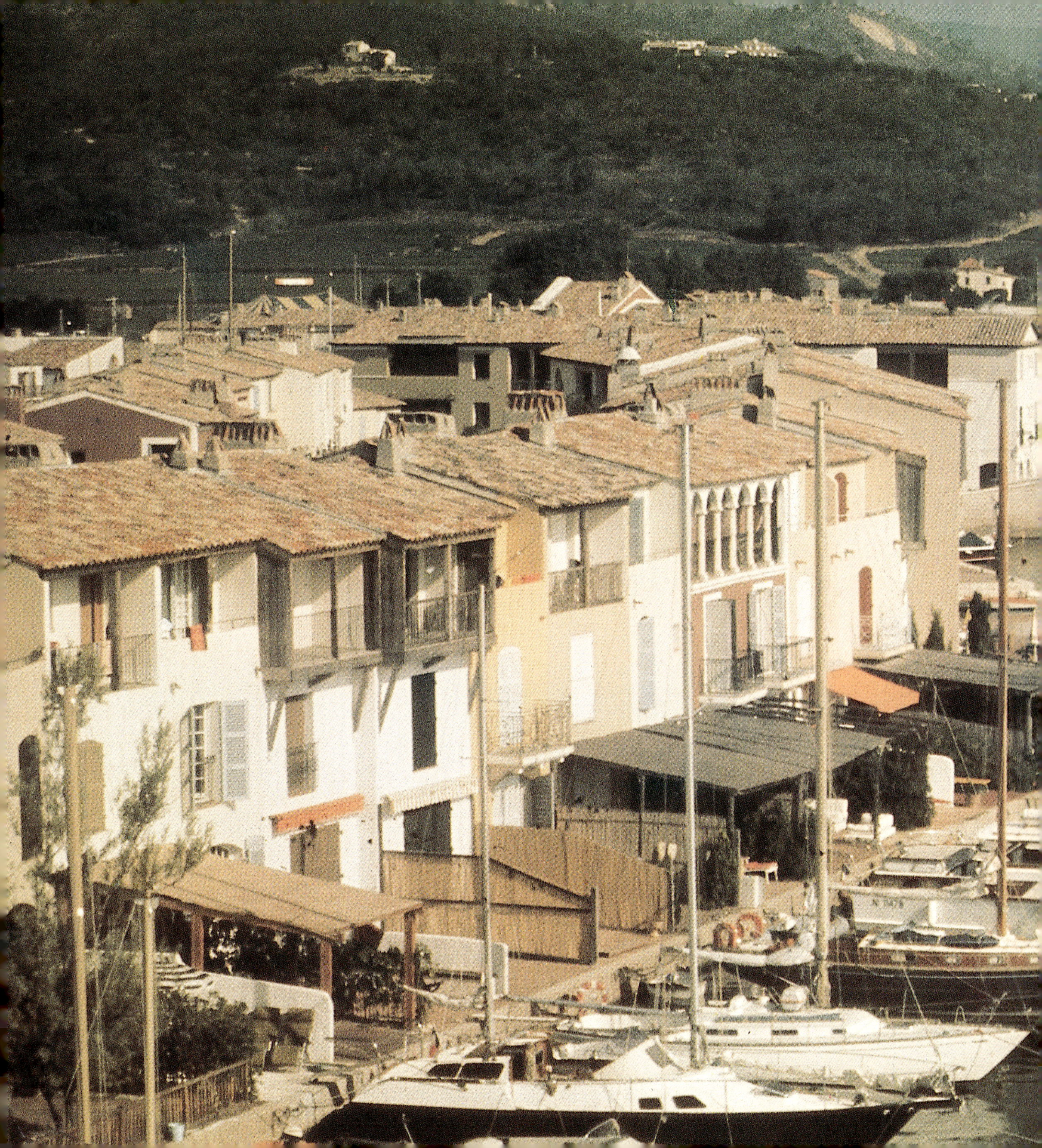

The village of Port Grimaud lies in a valley at the foot of the Mountains of Maures.

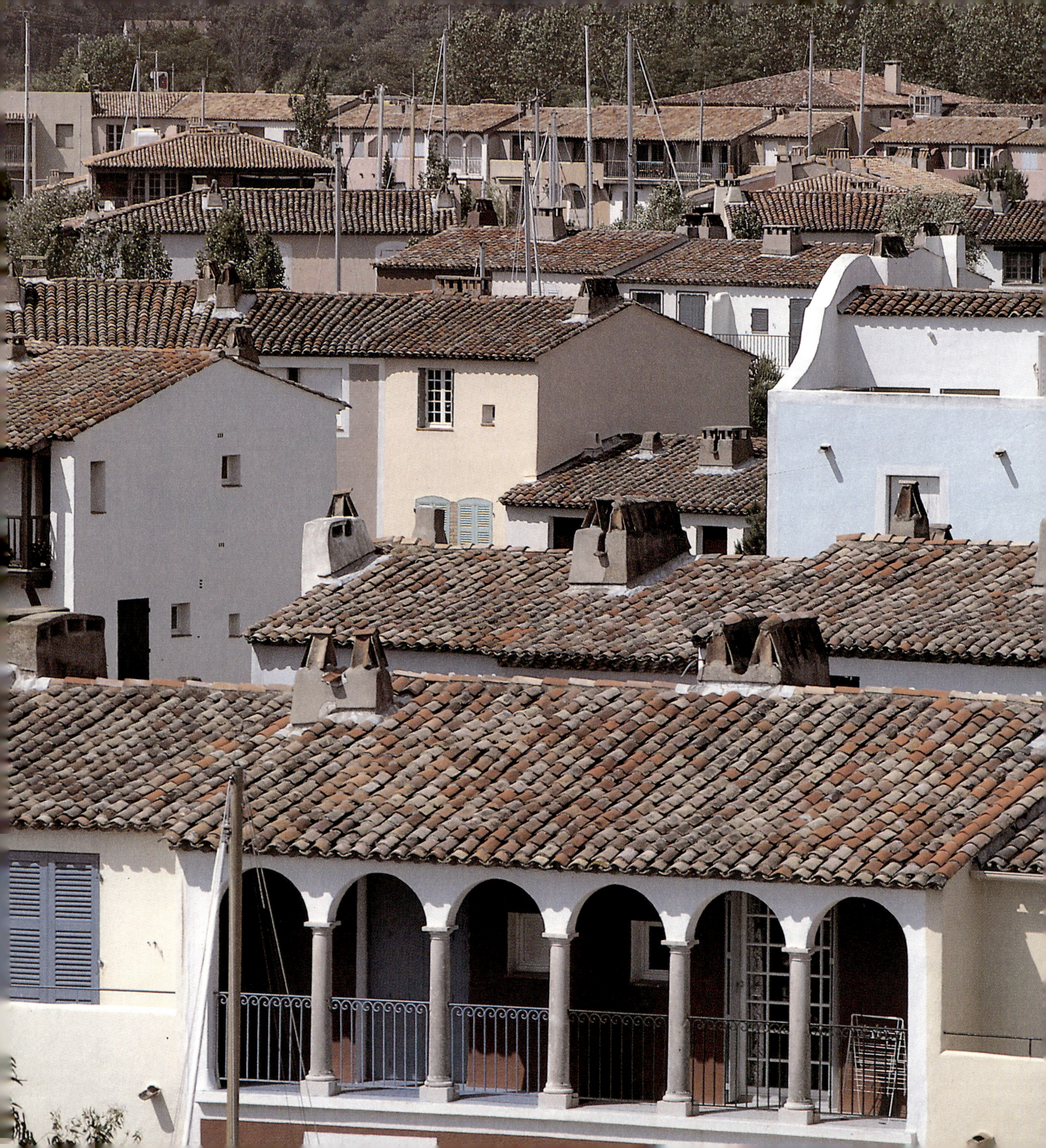

A Reassuring Architecture

In designing Port Grimaud I wanted to rediscover certain constants in scale, together with the feeling of permanence which belonged to the vernacular architecture I had so admired on my travels in Greece.

I also wanted to make a clear and unequivocal statement that a return to traditional and regional architecture can produce an authentic creation and not – as most of my critics affirmed, many of whom have never set foot in Port Grimaud – merely an imitation of the real thing.

"To learn about traditional towns", wrote the architectural historian Maurice Culot, *"means that to understand them one must study them and look on them as the real laboratories of the future, privileged places in which to reconquer a unique kind of culture.*

"In every process of this kind the method of creating is by initation; to blow the breath of life back into scholarly and creative concepts is, at one stroke, to rehabilitate many other categories which have been so unfairly defamed, the copy, the real art of the pastiche and, most difficult of all, the restoration of the original."

Jaques Rigaud in his book *A Cultural-Life Style* underlines the fact that from the time of the Roman Empire to a third of the way through the twentieth century, there was a creative continuity in every region, in every country.

Roman tiles play their part in achieving architectural unity and to the sense of harmony between the Port and charming old village of Grimaud some kilometres away up into the mountains.

Beneath the balcony of the Community Centre which is supported on wooden pediments, carried by stone columns, the water reflects the play of light and shade.

The massive churches of Martigues and Saintes-Maries-de-la-Mer inspired the design of the church at Port Grimaud.

This continuity, he says, applies as much to farms as it does to castles, houses, churches and public buildings. In continuity he sees enshrined one of the most profound manifestations of solidarity between popular culture and the culture of the élite. Maurice Culot's thinking stresses the vital point that we must at all costs prevent its loss. My colleagues and I, very conscious of the meaning of solidarity, tried to embody it in our many and varied projects.

Before designing Port Grimaud I did some exhaustive research and collected a vast amount of documentation on the architecture of Provence, Italy and Spain. I made a list of the formulae used by the builders of the past and we searched far and wide for old, ready-made components that we could incorporate into our work. In our search we salvaged some useful treasures, largely found on local demolition dumps, including old beams, flooring, roof-tiles and bits of wrought and cast-iron work.

The ambience of Port Grimaud, is one of timelessness. It came into being not only because of its affiliation with the past but because I used the traditional core, using a whole arsenal of equally traditional shapes, all of which gave me the possibility of creating a homogeneous whole, while diversifying the details. The methods of construction I chose allowed me a wide choice of pitches for the roofs. The structure of the facades, the positioning of the barely perceptible curves allow the sun to brush walls, to "light them up". These are the kind of unexpected details which the visitor happens to discover and which create the charm and character of a town.

The gently sloping roofs were covered with pastel-coloured Roman and Genoese tiles whose ochre and straw tints weathered by time are an ever-changing enchantment. By means of subtle interpretation we used the colours of Provencal vernacular architecture; the coats of paint which underline window frames and windows enhance the shadow of the tiles, the balconies and facades. All these factors contribute to the harmony of the whole. A harmony which owes much to the absence of disruptive elements such as TV aerials and telegraph poles. If at first the residents or visitors to Port Grimaud fail to notice that these adjuncts of the modern

This multi-coloured stained glass window is the work the artist Vasarely. It is the only source of natural light in the church. It demonstrates the happy union between traditional architecture and the work of a contemporary artist.

The 'place du Sud' with its ornamental fountain decorated with Portuguese tiles.

The 'place du Marché' and the 'place du Sud' are the two focal points of activity of this quarter of Port Grimaud. Boutiques and other small shops can be reached from both the canals and the square. Open air markets give the town its cheerful ambiance. Opposite are apartments decorated with cast-iron columns and balconies in wrought-iron which help give this area the look of New Orleans.

51

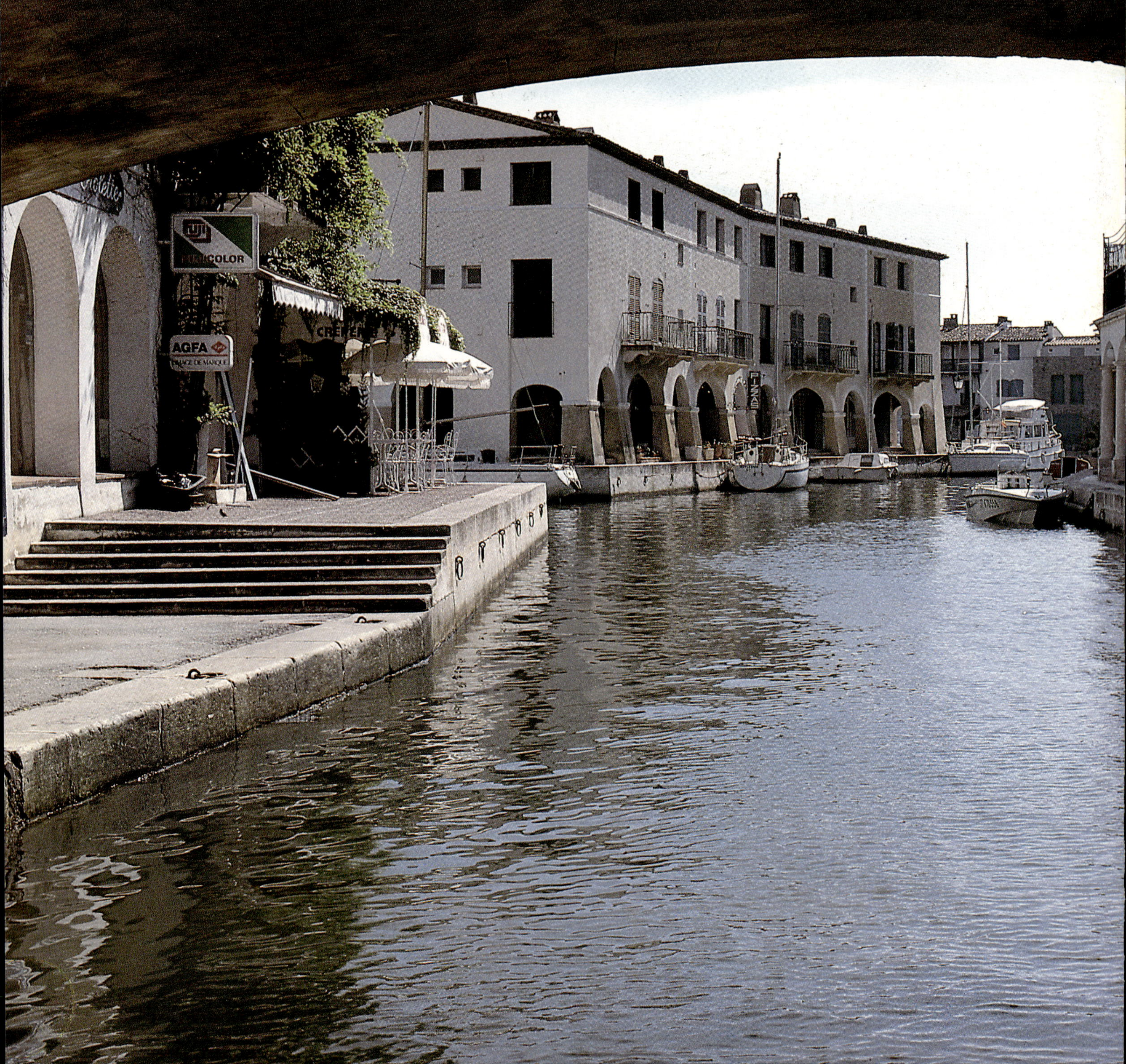
AGFA

world are missing, they will no doubt be conscious of a feeling of relief when they discover their absence. For the proliferation of these artefacts, which play so large a part in the contemporary life of so many French towns and villages, is a visual disaster. Underground galleries criss-cross the town. In them are housed all the mechanical and technical services considered indispensable to the comfort and convenience of the residents.

Gentle Architecture seeks to reassure, as well as to please. I wanted the streets to be the counter-point of the canals. That is why we designed special peep-holes giving glimpses of the seascape. Here and there we created little beaches where small boats can be pulled up out of the water. The gaps between the houses established pleasing vistas and perspectives. The streets, bordered by gardens, are dotted with charming and unusual architectural details each contributing to the general harmony of the whole. We pondered deeply over every detail of the design and made sure that our interpretation of what we created was appropriate to its particular setting – lanterns, lamp-posts, name-plates, benches and even the ground received careful attention. A good example is the pebble paving in the form of a mosaic in front of the shops in the Place du Marché. In the past the importance of detail used to be implicit in any architectural project. The work of Gabriel Davioud in Paris under the Second Empire is particularly significant. He was responsible for drawing Haussman's perspectives, as well as all the elements constituting the decor of the Parisian street. He designed lamp holders as well as the cast-iron cages that protect the trees; no detail was too small. The time had come, I felt, to return to this level of detail. I tried within reason to bestow the same care on Port Grimaud just as, some years earlier, I had paid special attention to the setting and life style of my first project in Mulhouse, for which I worked as both designer and builder, as I have mentioned earlier.

The 'canal du Nord', which is one of the narrowest
of Port Grimaud's many canals, has a distinctly
Venetian atmosphere. Its many restaurants add
a warm and welcoming touch.

At the end of the *'Isle Longue'* is François Spoerry's own home. Whenever he is at home he flies his flag from the flag pole on the Saracen tower.

Above, a sizeable house bordering the canals. Left, small appartment buildings on the place du Marché which are entered from the rear with their own staircases and verandas.

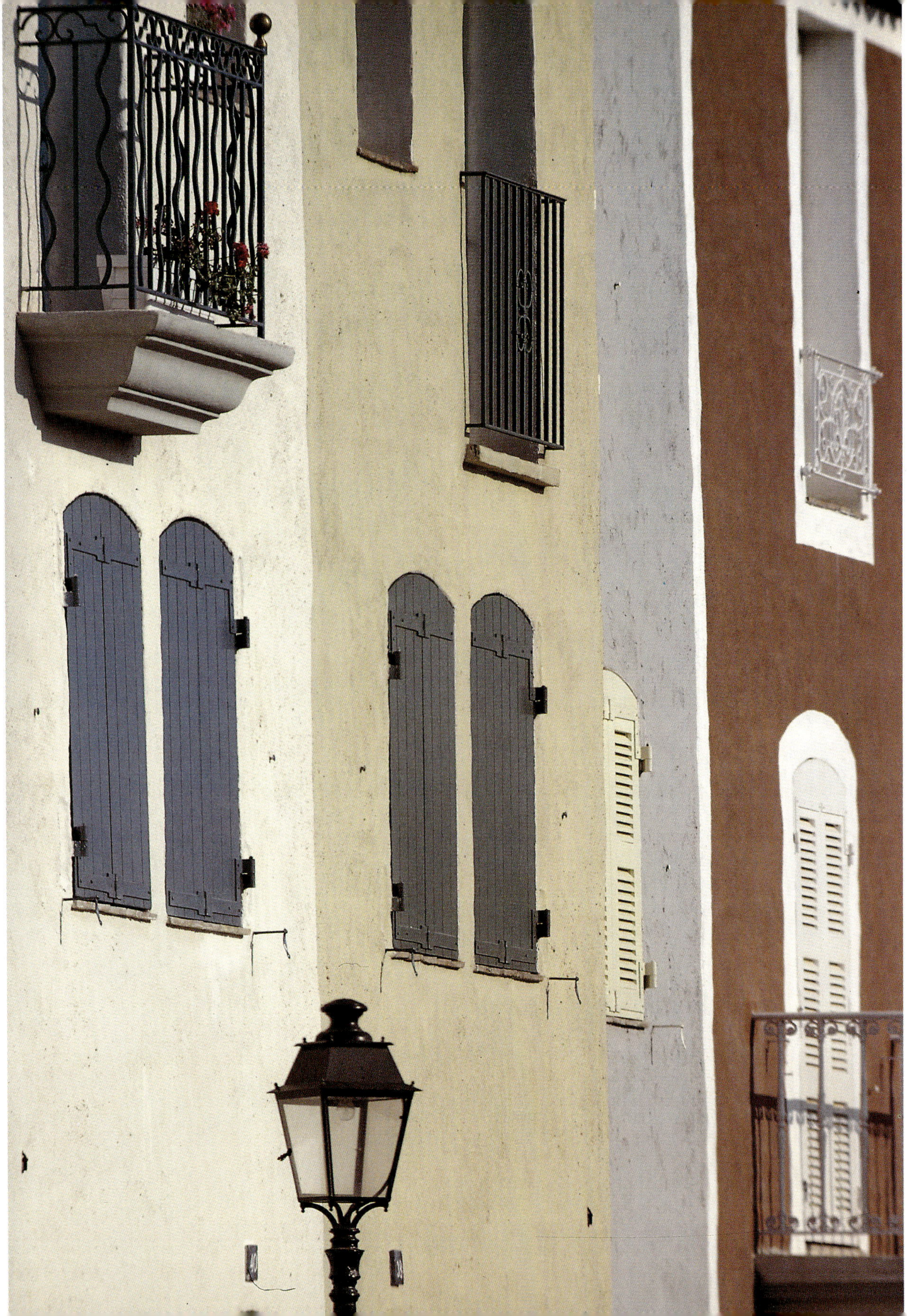

The Elements of a Gentle Architecture

I am, I believe, acutely sensitive to beauty and aesthetic quality but, even more, I am aware of the pleasure one receives from one's home surroundings. Since streets are the most extensive features of any town, I pay particular attention to the quality of their surroundings and their decoration – an essential part of the art of street-planning.

My colleagues and I attached particular importance to the vital living spaces designed specifically to give the impression of having been matured by time and exposure to the weather.

No practical reasons obliged us to make provision for pillars, fountains and frescoes, traditional features which help to bring a town to life, linking it with the traditions of the past, and so prevent it from being dull, or tedious.

The architect's responsibilities are not confined to the design of the town plan and the design of each of the buildings, they must also include very close consideration of, and attention to, detail and ornamentation.

Trompe-l'œil, ornaments and harmony of colour, all provide enchanting surprises for the passer-by to discover and delight in.
However, the sobriety of some forms is set off by the exuberant lushness of others.

At Port Grimaud I made good use of decorative columns, ornamental balconies, wrought-iron work, *trompe-l'œil*, painted tiles and pediments. I borrowed monumental doors, and archways from old towns. These distinctive entrances marked the boundary from one sector to another, underlining the transition from a public place to one that was semi-private, and thus creating oases of shade and coolness.

One may see in Port Grimaud porches, archways and doors forming part of the typology of the urban landscape and creating an event, an unusual aura of mystery and surprise. I wanted the visitor who usually wanders through the old parts of ancient cities hoping to come upon such examples of serendipity to find in Port Grimaud the same mysterious and delightful discoveries. It is old towns and villages that give a free rein to individual tastes, and to fantasy, which is deemed to be of capital importance. For as Jacques Rigaud wrote, *"If the town is not a little mad, then its inhabitants may well go crazy"*.

Among the components which go to make up a town, which traditionally lent itself to fantasy and surprises, one of the chief components was urban ornamentation. By creating festive landscapes, amusing and charming happenings and surprises, one was able to avoid boredom. In modern towns and cities we find ourselves in a theatre from which the scenery has been banished, leaving only the bare structure. I wanted to imbue Port Grimaud with a festive atmosphere, for embellishments are like a wink, a way of not taking oneself too seriously; they are one of the aspects of fantasy which inspire courtesy, good humour and a feeling of conviviality.

This was the spirit in which the frescoes which decorate the Place du Marché at Port Grimaud were painted. Among them is depicted the young woman, who from her balcony-window looks down with curious and amused gaze upon the stir and bustle of the town and the scenic qualities of the canals. It is not unusual in Provence or in Italy to find similar frescoed *trompe-l'œil*.

One of the masters of modern architecture, Frank Lloyd Wright, said "Embellishment is an integral part of architecture; it is to architecture what the flowering of a plant or tree adds to its structure. Embellishment produces an emotional reaction, and if it is correctly conceived, is not only akin to poetry, but is also the innate character of a structure uplifted, recaptured".

Those wanting to see merely a stage-set in the clusters of houses and buildings at Port Grimaud are precisely those persons responsible for the disappearance of all fantasy from the buildings in their towns and cities. If among followers of the modern movement there were architects who clamoured for a Cistercian austerity of style, and nobody has a higher regard for Cistercian architecture which derives from such talent and spirituality than I – but the fact is that the majority of post-war buildings which claimed to be severe and honed to the bone were in reality the result of a complete paucity of imagination.

The Americans have coined the word 'casual' to denote the architecture for day-to-day living, preoccupied as they are rather with the setting for their life style than for its grandeur. I would qualify this life-style as being "minor" (as opposed to "major") monumental architecture in the same way that one of Georges Brassens' songs is in complete contrast to Wagner's Ring Cycle. But Port Grimaud came into being before its time. Building it raised tremendous controversial issues which were furiously debated not only by the public, who from the start looked very favourably upon the enterprise, but also by the intelligentsia, accustomed to admiring the cultural commonplace.

Eventually, however, the undeniable success of the lagoon town caused some of its detractors to reverse their initial judgements and re-think their views of the art of building. This happened to the extent that I can now hope that Port Grimaud is seen to be one of the achievements produced in France and elsewhere in the world which may herald the genesis of a freer architecture, closer to the needs and wishes of the public, an architecture which will be part and parcel of the post-modern movement.

Achievements of Modern Architecture

The doctrine of the modern movement, having been totally accepted, are now totally rejected. Those who were slavishly dependent upon its tenets then began systematically to criticise, and even denigrate contemporary architecture. All the many post-modernist architects may well have brushed aside all that was forbidden and brought a new lease of life into the meaning of the word "creation" yet contemporary architecture has still – and I am the very last person to forget this – achieved some considerable successes.

I subscribe to some architectural expressions and to some degree of lyricism in modern architecture, and I also approve of displaying technical skills in the use of the various types of building materials, as long as they serve to make architecture fit in with specific functions. It would be impossible to list all such examples, but the following are particularly worth noting: Saarinen's TWA air terminal in New York, Roger Taillebert's Montreal grandstand, and the Bercy sports stadium by Andrault and Parat. I particularly admire the aesthetics of New York where what results are "surprise" scenic effects whose excitement and beauty are created by the overall effect of all the many sky-scrapers which tower over the city. These scenic effects are also the result of superb technical perfection which one cannot fail to admire.

Other significant feats of architecture are the magnificent works of Pei, one of whose greatest achievements is

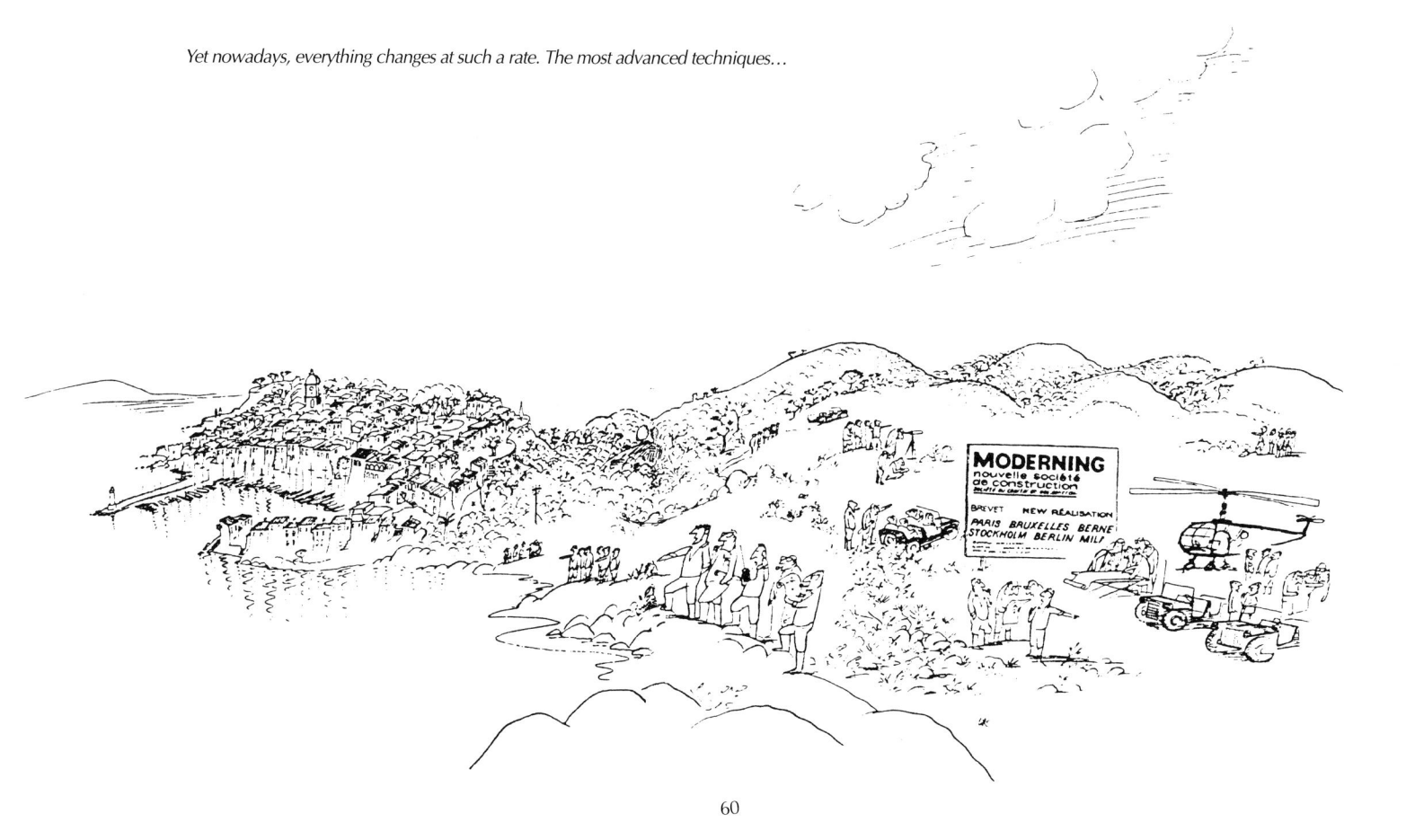

Yet nowadays, everything changes at such a rate. The most advanced techniques...

the new Museum of Modern Art in Washington. Pei is a first-class architect and a great designer, who pays the utmost attention to detail (one cannot produce great architecture unless the details are all absolutely flawless). Mies Van de Rohe had already made this point: "With architects like Pei, Skidmore, and a few other names, functionalism is ennobled with technological and technical perfection". From its very early stages, Pei's Cour du Louvre was a project which entirely convinced me. However, this project got a bad press. Nonetheless, a piece of architecture of good, sound quality, will hold its own against any other styles, as well as fitting in well with the general pattern of tradition. In France, up until a few years ago, there was a grave shortage of buildings of quality such as those one sees in the United States, which one cannot help but admire, such as the IBM building in New York by the firm of Skidmore, Owings and Merrill. In France, we have only a few such achievements of which to be proud. The Montparnasse Tower in Paris, for example, makes the point well: the tower does not fit in to its setting, it crushes everything without adding a thing to its surroundings, nor can one say that it glorifies the beauty all around it. I prefer Philip Johnson's style, an example of which can be seen in his building in Pittsburgh, a sublime structure in glass and steel with a hint of the neo-gothic of the early sky-scrapers.

In an attempt to find some examples of modern French architecture, one would perhaps attempt to find some sort of merit in the Paris quarter of La Défense, which is, by all accounts, inaccessible, and a total failure as an example of town-planning, both in the style of each revolving tower block, and of each and every basement. Although the actual site is an attractive one, all the buildings seem to lack depth and grandeur. There is no sense of majesty about the place, it has no quality. I detest its

...are used in creating

ridiculous pretentiousness, despite the fact that some of the buildings, such as the Nobel Tower by De Mailly, the Elf-Aquitaine building by Overcash, Julien and Saubot and also the Willerwal buildings, are of outstanding quality. Had I been asked to develop La Défense, I would have been inspired by the grid layout of New York. There would have been no revolving tower blocks but the roads would have been laid out at right-angles to one another. Having said that, it would have meant my entering a competition, something I have never done (which partly explains why, for a long time, I was a complete stranger and quite unknown in architectural circles, those elitist Parisian circles which have the power to promote an architect's reputation). To go back to the subject of La Défense, it stands to reason that I should see Otto von Spreckelsen's idea, that of a triumphal arch, as a totally marvelous solution. But what was the reasoning behind his decision to shift its axis by a few degrees? Did he do it in order simply to "be fashionable"?

No-one should be surprised if I say that I have never been a great follower of "fashionable" movements. Hence, I missed out on the beginnings of some Parisian firsts, which spear-headed architectural movements. I do not know the majority of my fellow architects personally, I know them only through those articles in the journals that I may happen to read. Some of them I admire, those who are thorough and strong and who can produce bold architecture, such as Andrault and Parat, Chemetov, Willerwal, Taillebert and Parent. I also deeply admire architects able to imbue their work with a sense of humour and with the spirit of creativity, such as Nunez or the Belgian, Krier, or Portzamparc for his highly imaginative style. Portzamparc was the first to cock a

…the most daring of modern styles.

snook at Le Corbusier's architecture. I knew and loved Fernand Pouillon. He and I travelled to Algeria together to see some of his work there. I share his opinion that fashions in the art of building are governed by cultural trends as well as a slow evolution of form. Nevertheless, the successful architectural work is one in which the personality of its creators is reflected in the work rather than its being derived wholly from some theory or other. The vast majority of architects have remained inflexible in their work which sadly lacks wit and humour.

The use of technical forms of expression is something of which Norman Foster is a great exponent. As far as I can see, this term signifies expressing non-existent functions by use of artificial means. An example of this can be seen in the tower blocks of Hong Kong. On that score, Nouvel, in his work for the Arab World Institute, reveals a more exciting style (I had already had the chance to admire this architect's expressionist tendencies in his work on the renovation of the Belfort theatre). I also greatly admire the aggressive side of Venturi's styles and have respect for some Parisian architecture. I would like to mention the example of the block on the Avenue Matignon by Mazzuconni. On the facade of the curtain wall, which fits in well between the neighbouring buildings, there is a section of wall resembling either a nearby building, or perhaps a tower block which might once have stood there. This amusing detail is restrained, harmless, and in good taste. In that tower block the architect created an example of fine town-planning, something one might like to have seen during those dark years of architecture, which are, I hope, behind us!

during those dark years of architecture, which are, I hope, behind us!

Now that freedom has been gained, every kind of style, some at variance with each other, seem now to be quite normal, even natural.

But when I started work at Port Grimaud, it was very rare to find architects with sufficient courage to break away from the well beaten paths of the Modern Movement in architecture. A notable exception was Ricardo Bofill, whose style and quality of work, I deeply admire.

My reaction to today's architecture is usually emotional; I am a pragmatist and do not believe in analysis. In my opinion, analysing is something one does when there is no room to synthesize or to be creative. Too many people these days look upon analysis as a means to an end (thus relieving them of any obligation to take action and distancing them from reality).

The active life I have always led has stopped me from pouring over matters intellectual. I am, first and foremost, a man of action with a decided taste for risks. Offices and studios are not to my taste. It is my belief, and one I share with the architectural critic, Charles Jencks, that when discussing post-modern architecture, that the analysis of architecture must never deter the architect from his efforts to communicate, this enables the architect to meet the public.

The drawings on pages 64, 65 and 66
are by Sempé, they were published in
L'Express in 1969.

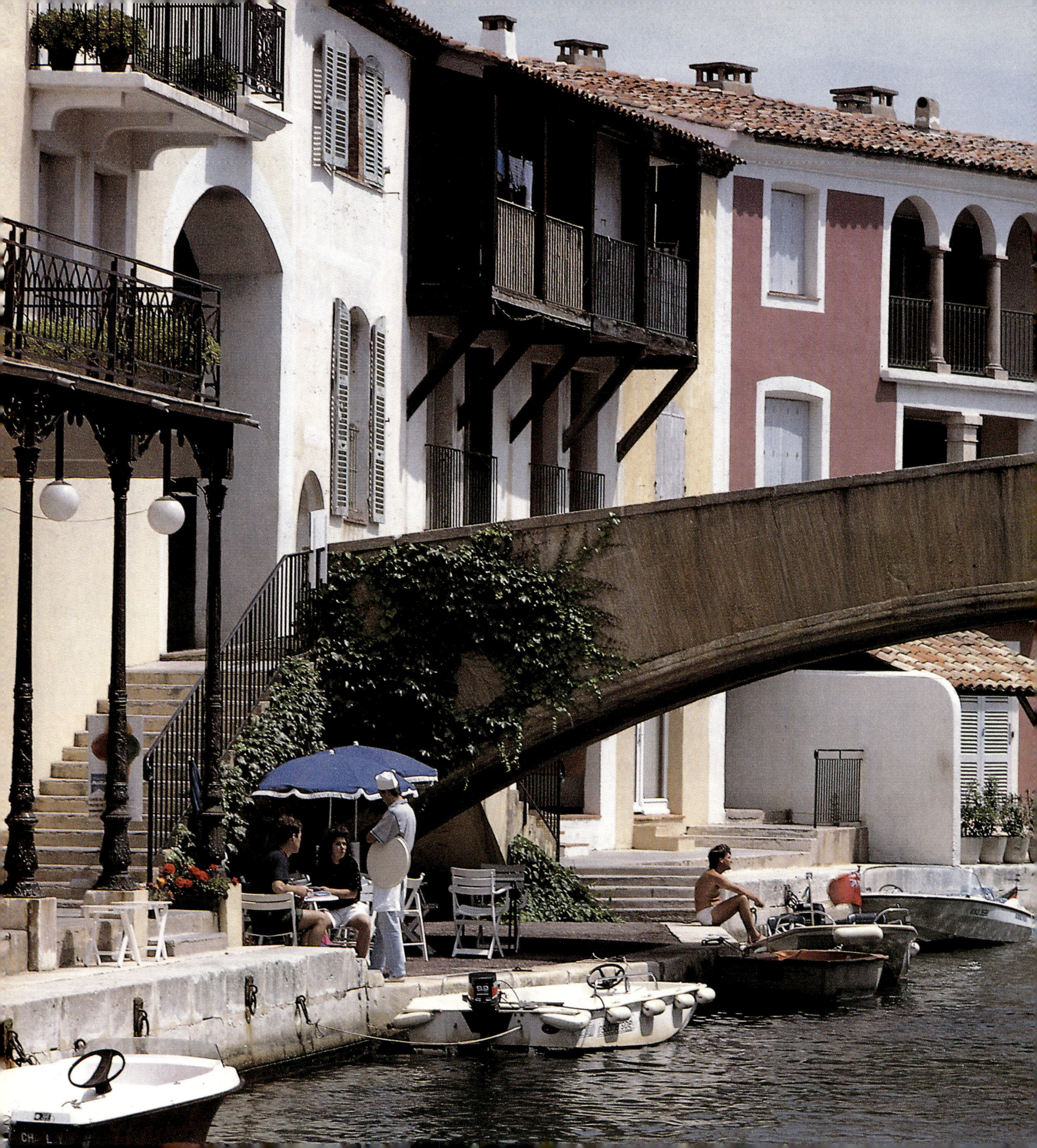

Architecture, A Most Public Language

Architecture as a language for the public – is one of the key notions of post-modernist architecture. It stresses three elements equally: continuity of the urban fabric, ornamentation and symbolism.

At the beginning of 1985, an exhibition was organised at the George Pompidou Centre in Paris, entitled *The New Pleasures of Architecture*; it featured the trends which have dominated design since the seventies. The exhibition reflected a new state of mind. It expressed the shattering shift in mentality which has occurred within a very short span of time and in which developments such as those at Port Grimaud are now, I hope, not seen to be too strange. The title of the exhibition was in itself significant. At last, one could speak openly of the "pleasures of architecture", a proof of the extraordinary liberation throughout the world of architecture, of the blossoming forth of personalities and of talent seen from different angles and expressed through different languages. This phenomenon can only bring rejoicing to those who had for a considerable time been longing for some reaction against the conventional and who advocated the need for more sources of inspiration and forms. Let us hope that this new architecture will succeed in avoiding all the traps of the past and that its representatives will not condemn outright, all modern architecture including that designed by architects of talent.

Like Venice, the canals are the natural thoroughfares. They combine all the advantages of being both practical, pleasant as well as fast.

According to Maurice Culot, post-modernist architecture uses irony, ambiguity, historic and vernacular interpretation. All these allow post-modernist architecture to be understood by the experts and accepted by the public. In addition, the public can rediscover in these buildings historical references rooted in times past. Post-modernist architecture is an exciting and liberating adventure. Rid of the dogmatism which had broken with the collective memory, and therefore with popular opinion, it has now regained the favour of the public. This delights me, since it means that architecture is once again considered to be a pleasure. Today, pluralism, eclecticism, a taste for decoration no longer shock. The new generations of builders who take their inspiration from creations which had made an important impact on the history of architecture, are infinitely more sensitive than those who are not similarly inspired. Buildings which resemble those around them are more powerful than those which have nothing in common.

Architecture is an art of communication, it is not merely a language of technicians; it also needs the added ingredient of lyricism. If the Rialto bridge in Venice is a theatre in which each and every individual discovers with rapture, then the bridges and monumental gates of Port Grimaud too are worthy of such poetic usage of space; it was for this very purpose that they were designed. Faced with the tremendous pace of contemporary living, and the fact that changes occur with ever-increasing speed, man needs to find a mooring from which he can weigh anchor. Architecture must also act as a source of reassurance, something which is absolutely necessary for a well-balanced society. In our subconscious lurks the need to seek out an environment which

In the building of the many bridges, as in the case of the houses, the architect played with a variety of forms, building materials and forms of ornamentation.

is similar to that of our childhood, therefore the real town must somehow reflect an enchanted town, whose image may come either from those childhood memories or from our imagination. Building a functional construction and creating a harmonious piece of town-planning are based on two entirely different precepts. The former is not created for the benefit of man who thirsts for the unexpected, and for a sense of variety.

> "Tell me, since you are sensitive to the impacts of architecture, have you not noticed as you stroll through the town, that among all the buildings which constitute the town, some are dumb, some talk, while others, and they are much rarer, sing. It is the talent of their creator or perhaps it may ever be the influence of the Muses. Buildings which neither speak nor sing deserve to be scorned, for they are dead things and of less importance in the hierarchy to those piles of rubble thrown from the backs of the lorries of building contractors."

These words, gaven to Phèdre in *Eupalinos and the Architect* by Paul Valéry, I have made my own. At Port Grimaud and on the other sites on which we are working we want to create *an architecture which will sing.*

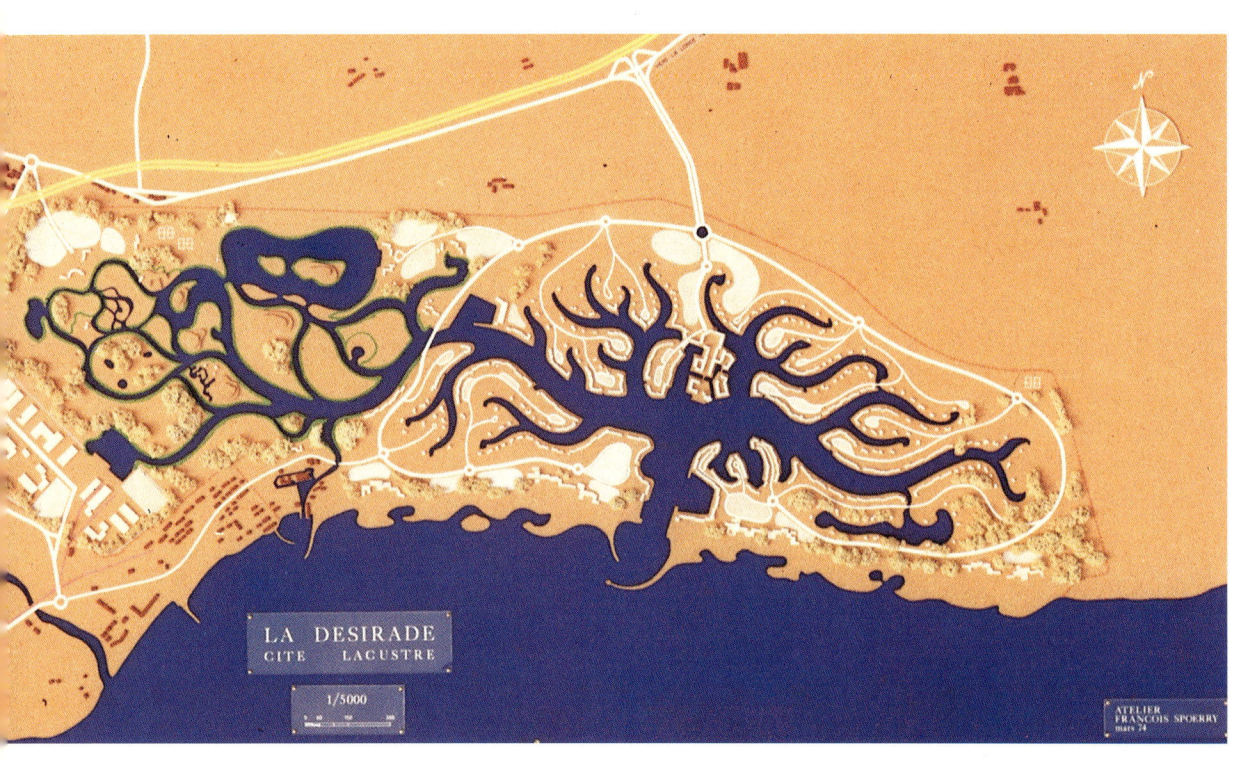

La Désirade, Hyères, designed in 1974. On a site of 350 hectares (approximately 700 acres) consisting of salt marshes between the coast and the main road a design was commissioned for a lagoon city with a centre for water sports together with a small industrial zone in which it proposed to site a shipyard and ship repairer.

Senlis, designed in 1972. This commission applied the form of the canals of Port Grimaud to a town on dry land. These became areas of greenery.

In the field of leisure, in which most of my activities are concentrated, rare are the designs founded upon a desire to achieve harmony with its site.

Our coastline has become disfigured by too many resorts. I need only mention the development of the Languedoc coastline where, although I quite readily accept that it has certain qualities in common with the Grande Motte, where Jean Balladur rejected aridity in favour of a touch of Baroque lyricism; or the quality of Port-Camargue, which comes very close to the urban concept of Port Grimaud; or of Cap d'Agde, where Jean Le Couteur made use of a gentle human style of architecture of which the depth and choice of materials do not have that aggressiveness which often serves as a foil, and this despite the few successes which are attributable to the architects' talent rather than that of the town-planners. I believe that the Languedoc-Roussillon operation is a complete disaster. Here the technocrats have systematically destroyed the natural areas of land while showing a complete lack of intelligence in their designs of new urban complexes: enchanting towns like Leucate or Gruissan, which were ravishing, did not deserve to wake up to the new surroundings inflicted upon them. There, the extensive and unrestricted powers of the Administration are apparent; its hand can be seen in the untimely dredging of the waters and the layout of buildings without due consideration being given to the wind protection factor. The site was of no apparent interest to the technocrats who were intent solely on misguidedly imposing their grandiose and prestigious images. And what is more, the influence of an architect-cum-town-planner such as Georges Candilis when associated with this virulent imposition of technical infrastructure, is, I feel, highly debatable.

Dreams and Realities

At the time, the Management Team for the Development of Languedoc invited me to consider developing the Gruissan site in the dual roles of architect and developer. However, when it was finally decided that I should only work on half the site, I turned the offer down as the half upon which I would have worked could never have had any credibility.

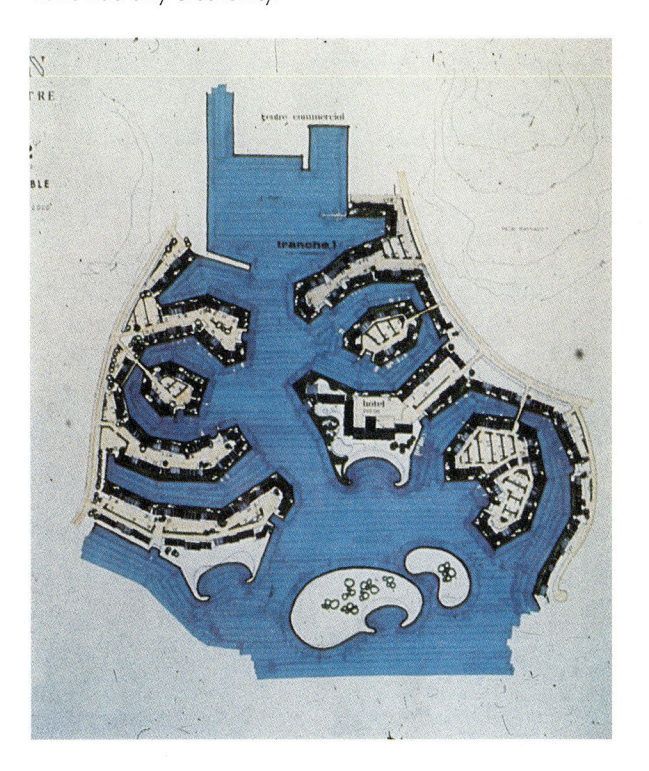

Gruisssan, designed in 1972. In building a lagoon port on land surrounding the ancient village of Gruissan, the task was not only to create a lagoon style port inspired by the local vernacular architecture but also of wholly integrating the existing village with its new port.

In an attempt to prevent Gassin from simply becoming a town entirely made up of second homes and so as to avoid wholly anarchic town-planning from taking over, the commune of Gassin, which borders the communes of Saint-Tropez, Cavalaire and Port Grimaud, resolved to build a modern extension to the medieval town. The houses in the new quarter were intended to be lived in only by families who work in the commune itself or in its immediate vicinity.

Cogolin, 1987. The problem of extending the village of Cogolin was resolved by designing an entirely new quarter on the edge of the village whose streets follow the same winding patterns of those of the older village.

The Golf Course at Gassin, 1983. A further example of the way in which buildings can blend into their surroundings.

Whereas at the Golf Course at Gassin, the problem involved placing forty-five thousand square metres of living space without destroying the site. The buildings consequently cover only a quarter of the surface area of the golf course and are no taller than the height of the trees.

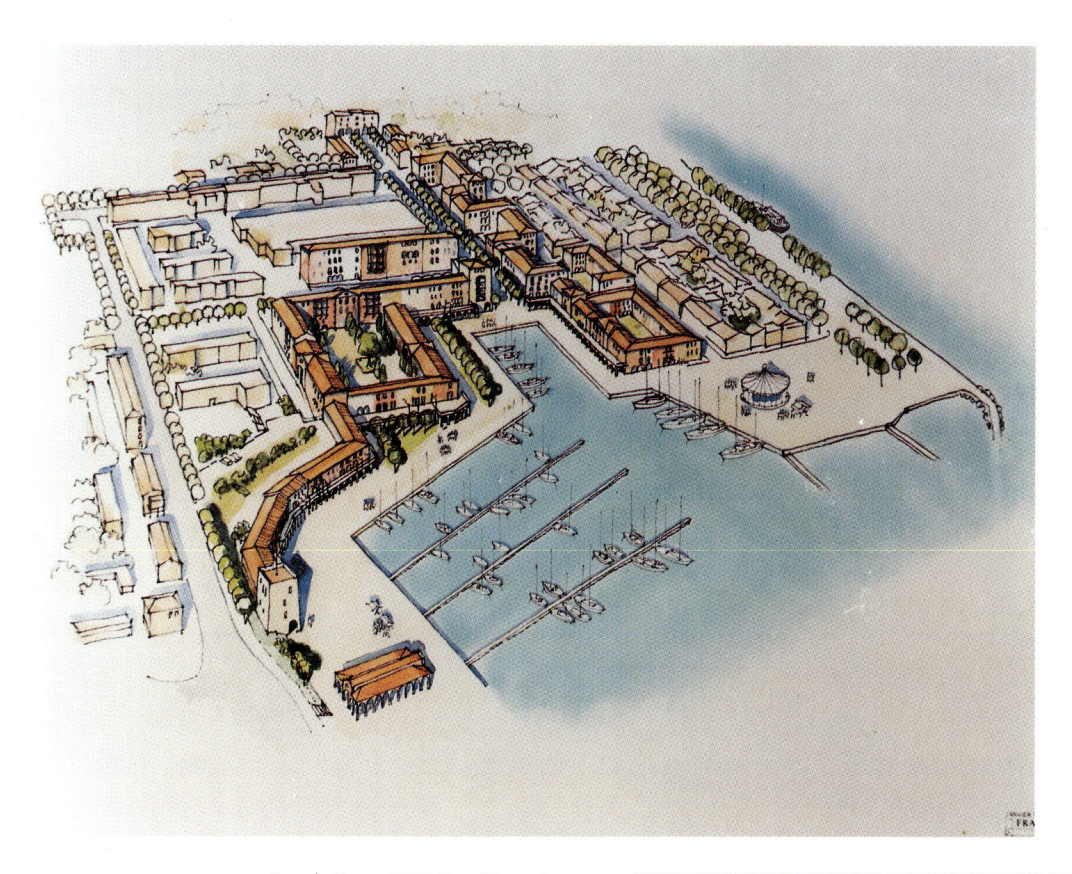

Port-de-Bouc, 1987. The shipyard which once stood at the centre of the town was forced to close due to a falling order book. It is planned to replace it with a new centre to the town overlooking a marina. The architecture and urban planning necessary for the new centre are designed to complement that which already exists.

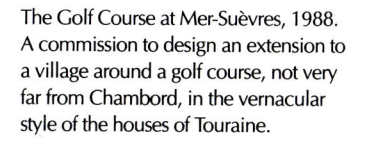

The Golf Course at Mer-Suèvres, 1988. A commission to design an extension to a village around a golf course, not very far from Chambord, in the vernacular style of the houses of Touraine.

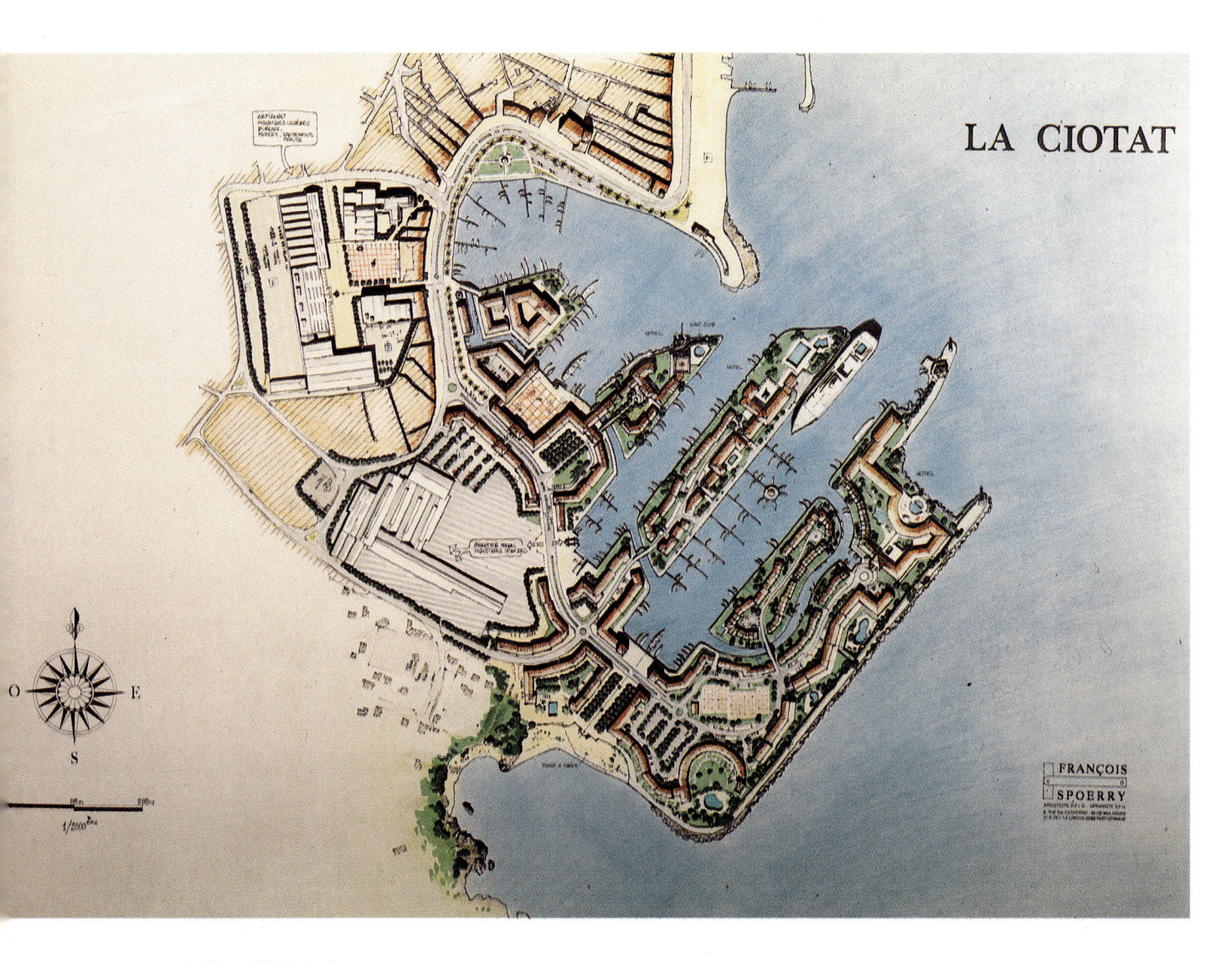

La Ciotat, 1987 – In plan.

With the cooperation of some of the town's most prominent citizens, we submitted plans to the town council for developing the industrial estate and the port area of La Ciotat so as to form an extension of the old town and at the same time create a large market-place, a conference centre, a marina, a maritime museum, three hotels, a landing wharf for liners and above all, a boatyard, as a way of sustaining a local industry in the form of the biggest specialist boatyard in the Mediterranean handling repairs to yachts and pleasure craft.

First and second homes, in the style of the houses of Port Grimaud are proposed around the edges of the harbour and along the banks of the canals.

The Golf Course at Roquebrune-sur-Argens, 1988. Contrary to the design of the golf course at Gassin, second homes and a hotel complex were placed at the centre of this golf course.

74

At Port Léman in Haute-Savoie, a group of villas and small blocks of flats (about five hundred flats) skirt the fringes of a marina and a small boatyard. The layout and aspect of the buildings, the interpenetration of nature into the village, the height of the houses, choice of materials and the choice of forms and volumes are all matters dictated by the site and by the typically vigorous characteristics of the vernacular architecture of Savoie with its high roofs with dormer windows, little side windows, gables and balconies. The Port Léman project, however, has been delayed due to the discovery of a bronze-age lagoon city at the site. Excavation work is currently in progress.

Model and elevations of Port-Léman in the commune of Champs-sur-Léman, Haute Savoie, 1986.

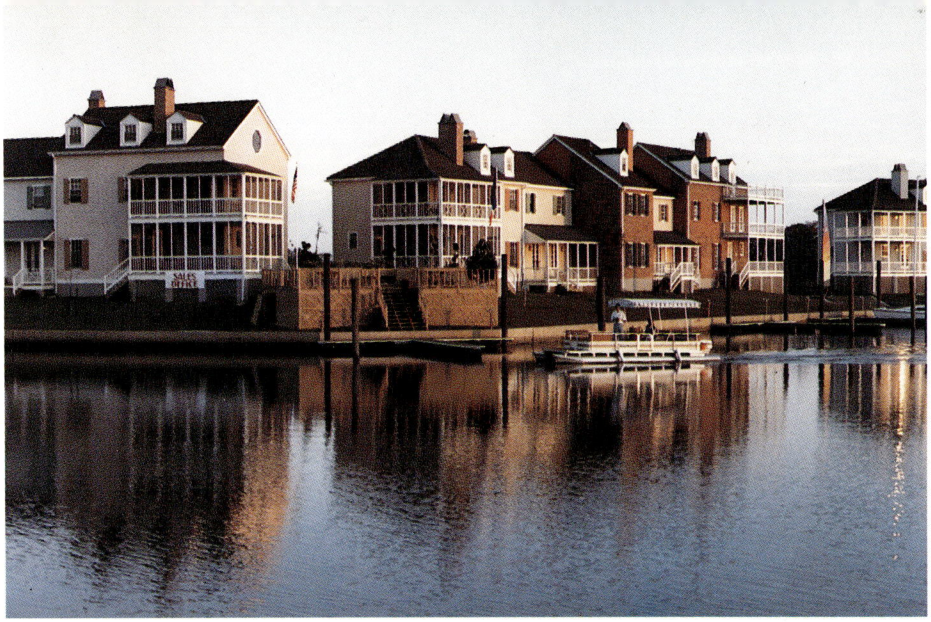

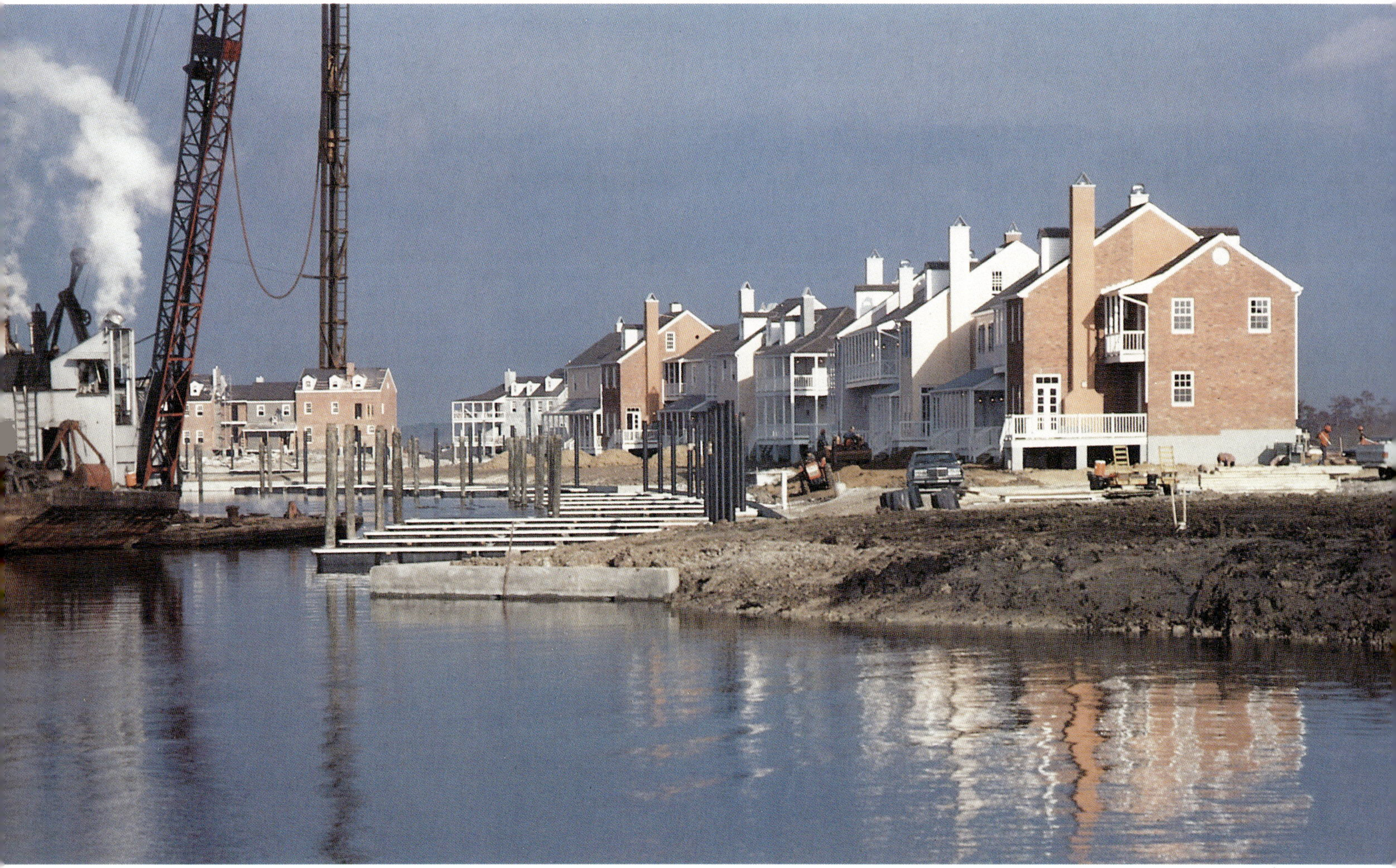

The project for Port Louis, Louisiana, in the United States, was at the design stage in 1981 and though building began on the site in 1984 (the first sixty houses had been completed by the spring of 1985) it has now ground to a halt on account of the slump in the economy of the State of Louisiana which has been brought about by a fall in the price of oil which in turn has ruined the region.

Port Louis is an expanse of marshy grassland covering 120 hectares. It is absolutely flat and surrounded on three sides by water. Over the past few years this marchland has been drained, but cars cannot travel over the ground due to the considerable risk of sinking into the marsh. This problem was all the more serious as it was impossible to use bulldozers. With Georges Giraud, with whom we had already worked at Port Grimaud, we came up with the solution by designing a very light machine, a kind of floating power-driven shovel. It was mounted on tracks which moved easily over the soil, and it could almost float on the shifting ground. However, safe tracks were needed for the lorries. So, on top of the sections of the site reserved for the roads, we laid a layer of plastic reinforced with fibreglass, followed by a layer of sand brought in by our power-driven shovel. Our "club sandwich" was laid to a depth of one metre. Even today, large lorries of over 20 tonnes continue to use these roads without difficulty. Eventually, as the land became a gigantic sponge, the marshy ground had to be drained completely to a depth of 1.50 metres and the water discharged into canals.

The architecture of Port Louis, once again drew its inspiration from the abundance of local architectural traditions which were dominated by the influences of Spanish and French settlers of the XVIth and the XVIIth centuries, together with English influences, in addition to the flowering of the Greek-Revival style of the XIXth century. It also borrows traditional features from the towns of southern Louisiana and from the tropics generally – covered verandas keep the rooms cool and shelter the inhabitants from the rain without forcing them to retreat indoors. The charm and elegance of the ante-bellum mansions of the plantations, such as those described in Maurice Denuzière's novels were bound to be commemorated with a hotel carrying his name and built in the style of the great houses owned by the old Southern aristocracy.

At the heart of the town, opposite the great circular basin commanding the entrance from the lake to the canals, was to be created a square, closed on three sides by buildings and arches. The fourth side, open to the water, was intended as the main quay for larger vessels. Shops were to be built sheltered by arcades, an eminently Hispanic setting of the kind one would expect to find in towns right across Latin America and at New Orleans in the "Vieux Carré". This ties in with one of my most enduring convictions – I am a firm believer in local shops, and shopping locally. The big chain stores are largely to blame for the dehumanising of towns, and for the changes that have occurred in the ways in which people behave towards one another. supermarkets are, in the main, anonymous places in which the pleasant dialogue between seller and buyer has disappeared, effectively inhibiting any sense of feeling that one either feels at ease in one's surroundings, or belongs to a community. The disappearance of these day-to-day contacts has contributed, to my mind, very greatly to the spread of aggressive and selfish behaviour which is so rapidly becoming the norm. In all our projects we force ourselves to increase the space for shops, thus bringing people together, enlivening a town and endowing it with charm.

Port Louis, Louisiana, photographed in 1985.
The houses of this lagoon city, which is built on piles, on the shores of Lake Pontchartrain, near New Orleans, are in the vernacular style of Louisiana in particular, and the tropics in general, an extremely rich tradition with many features from the Colonial period. Their shaded verandas dispense with the need for air conditioning.

Before deciding that they wanted me as their architect, representatives of the Mexican Government visited the Côte d'Azur and made a special trip to Port Grimaud. They were so favourably impressed that, since 1984, they have invited me to work on two projects for them: Cancún and Puerto Escondido.

Cancún, which is situated on the East Coast of the Yucatan peninsular in the Caribbean, is built on the edge of a coral reef, and is a typical example of the linear town-planning of the sixties. Built along a stretch of twenty or so kilometres it consisted of a scattering of large hotels and houses placed randomly across the available sites.

To give their geometrically designed yet disparate city the coherence it lacks, it was necessary to create a centre and a port. Between the Mexican town of Cancún and the zone in which the international hotels were situated, lies a flat area of marshy land covering three hundred and fifty hectares. Fonatour, the official organisation responsible for developing facilities for the Mexican tourist industry, allotted us this piece of land so as to complete the existing town. We designed a lagoon city which would form the heart of Cancún's urban complex. On a central island, opposite a vast well-protected inland port, public buildings will be built: a town hall, church and museum, as well as hotels and a yacht club. The scale of these buildings will be in keeping with the size of the port, an important stop-over route to the Caribbean Islands. Around a large arcaded square there will be a *"socaló"* (a characteristically Mexican park with its own church, community buildings and hotels) from which streets and alleys will branch off and in the same way the canals branch off from the large internal lake. The architecture here will be strongly influenced by the Hispano-Baroque tradition, which has given Mexico so many examples whose charm and imagination is incomparable.

Cancún, Yucatan, Mexico, 1984. The task given us by the Mexican Government was to create the heart of a spectacular new town to accomodate 70,000 inhabitants together with its own port on a site of 350 hectares from quite disparate elements.

Hotels border the Caribbean seafront, while the new town centre with its narrow canals and its arcaded buildings recalls certain aspects of Venice whilst also providing a marina and housing for both residents and visitors.

QUINTANA ROO
PUERTO CANCUN

FACHADAS SOBRE EL MAR

Puerto Escondido, Mexico, 1984. The city centre, with its church and city hall, was inspired by the Mexican Colonial style, with its streets on a grid-iron, and a *socalo*. An open-air theatre marks the starting point for the principal axis of the city, the long tree-lined avenue which runs down to the port's principal quay at which larger vessels will anchor.

The development of the site at Puerto Escondido on the Sea of Cortez, in Mexico, is one of the world's most ambitious projects in the field of leisure. Puerto Escondido was chosen by Mexican consultants with the agreement of the President of the Republic of Mexico to become a development that would offer facilities to an international standard, thereby generating much needed revenues to boost the country's economy. The close proximity of the United States seems to guarantee the project's success: Puerto Escondido is only one hour's flying time from Los Angeles.

The basic infra-structure of the city is almost complete. Its quays, streets and avenues have already been laid out. The city, which is designed for 200,000 inhabitants, is made up of a city centre running down to the harbour, and a number of discrete quarters or villages, some of which are sited by the shore, others on the surrounding hillsides, some indeed on the very tops of the hills themselves.

It covers an area of six thousand four hundred hectares. It is a greenfield site of great natural beauty. Subdivided by creeks and coves, it is closely overshadowed by mountain ranges rising to a height of over two thousand metres. In an attempt to avoid altering or disturbing an area of such outstanding natural beauty, we devised a somewhat unusual piece of town planning: except in a few authorized sectors, all building will be forbidden. This plan, which has the approval of both Fonatour and the Mexican Government, ensures that future villages in Puerto Escondido, which will come to constitute the various quarters of the future city. The city, which will have an estimated population of two hundred thousand inhabitants, will be built on the seashore, on the hillsides, and high enough above the sea-level to provide quite spectacular views; fishing villages will nestle deep within the creeks, fortress towns, and other fortress-type villages will be built under the peaks on mountain slopes. We saw to it that the villages will appear as an extension of the escarpments upon which they are built. Colours, materials and overall composition will make certain that these villages blend in with the mountains; simple in design, the buildings are again inspired by local tradition, this is shown by the numerous terraces and the use of different levels.

The heart of the complex, where work started in 1986, is sited at the entrance to a magnificent, natural bay, more than three kilometres wide. This is Puerto Escondido, the "hidden port". It is linked to the open sea by a narrow channel and closely surrounded by small islands whose hillsides slope very steeply.

The orthogonal plan of the city centre resembles the plan of an ancient Mexican town of the Aztec period. The Spanish conquerers of the XVIth century adopted and adapted this plan, and the most marked urban features of their architecture clearly evokes the style of building of the Colonial period. In the past, the prominence of siting and the quality of construction was always clearly indicative of the particular function of public buildings. I, therefore, felt that the design of the public buildings at Puerto Escondido must remain within this tradition. Its established image as a city whose buildings are of monumental size and

This quarter of Puerto Escondido will be the centre of a fortress village. Perched on the sides of a hill, it draws its inspiration from the adobe style of architecture of New Mexico.

At Puerto Escondido, the port was designed in the shape of an elipse, bordered by arcaded buildings and dominated by the City Hall, whose architecture is typically Mexican.

(On the opposite page) Away from the city centre, the architecture becomes far less sophisticated and evoking that of Mexican coastal villages.

importance and have great decorative richness, constituting important stylistic features. Elements characteristic of the architecture of the Colonial Baroque, with its rich detail, were used with discretion: ornamental facades, columns, arcades, loggias, patios, decorative details, colours, geometric forms all give diversity so as to always avoid banality. In a site as exceptional as that of Puerto Escondido uniformity would be quite intolerable. The Mexicans, proud of the past and of their cultural heritage, to which this project faithfully adheres, have given us both their total support and also a completely free hand.

In the immediate vicinity of the city centre will lie the lagoon city. The houses, built on the peninsulas, will all have their own private moorings, and a hotel will be built in the prime position overlooking the entrance to the main canal. Behind the lagoon city, on the flat parts of the site, provision has made for a golf course whose fairways will be bordered by villas. Among other amenities, the leisure facilities will include a racecourse.

One must not forget to mention Puerto Escondido's most up-to-date facilities: an airport which will serve the whole area. The city will also be equipped with a cable network linked with data banks, permitting residents to do most of their day-to-day shopping by telephone.

To the seaward side of the city is the marina and the corniche, whereas on the lagoon city side of Puerto Escondido, the houses covered in their terraces, offer, as Port Grimaud has always done, a very warm welcome to both residents and their boats.

85

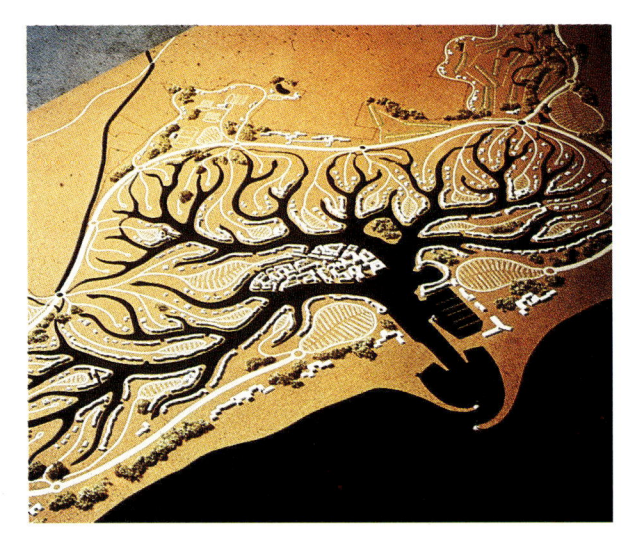

At Port Levant on the Costa Brava, I had made provision for four to five thousand apartments bordering the canals. This ambitious project was planned to cover five hundred hectares, while the design of the canals was to be inspired by the shape of a river and its tributaries. Apart from its aesthetic qualities, the project was based on a new formula which, by providing a more efficient water-flow system, would avoid the pollution of the canals. However, for political reasons this project, conceived in 1974 and 1975, never got off the ground.

Both above, at Port-Levant, Costa Brava, Spain, 1974, and below right at Djerba, Tunisia, 1973, the notion of a river and its tributaries underlies the design for the network of canals of these two lagoon cities.

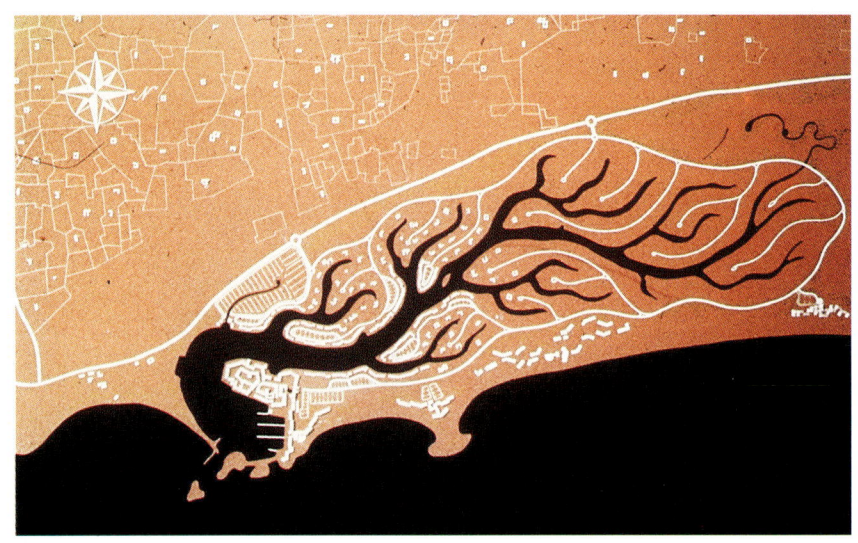

Model of a design for Puerto Careyes, Mexico, 1980.

On the west coast of Mexico, a small lagoon city, Puerto Careyes, was to occupy a site made somewhat unenticing both by the local topography and by the great surge of the Pacific. This deep bay, protected from the ocean by a high and naturally steep spur, meant that the houses on the banks would have to border a stretch of inland water. Alternatively, they could have been built in villages or hamlets clinging to the hillside. In this very beautiful setting, the dwellings would have had double aspects, with views over the port, and over the open sea. This project has yet to see the light of day.

Vilaricos, Spain, 1987. This triple project involved building a golf course, a lagoon city and a large extension to a village in the hills above a new port in Southern Spain. The creation of hill top villages which appear fortified, in the style and tradition of the villages of Andalusia, gives rise to particular interest in this design.

Port Lisa, Saint Martin, The French Antilles, 1988. The colonial style of this design derives from the vernacular architecture of the French Antilles which stresses, in particular, the use of large shady verandas which, in turn, minimises the need for air conditioning.

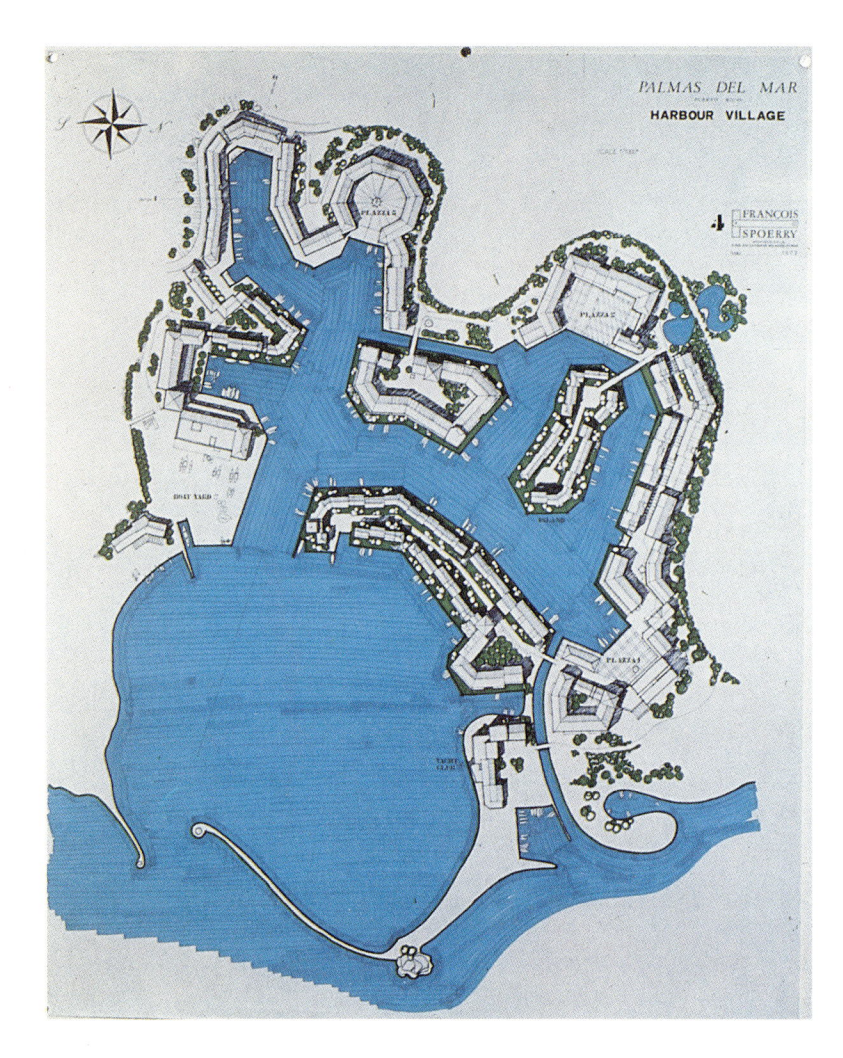

Jakarta, Indonesia, 1984. This study for an offshore artificial island is the reverse of the preceding projects, since the spoil from dredging the channels was used to form the penisulas upon which houses would then be built.

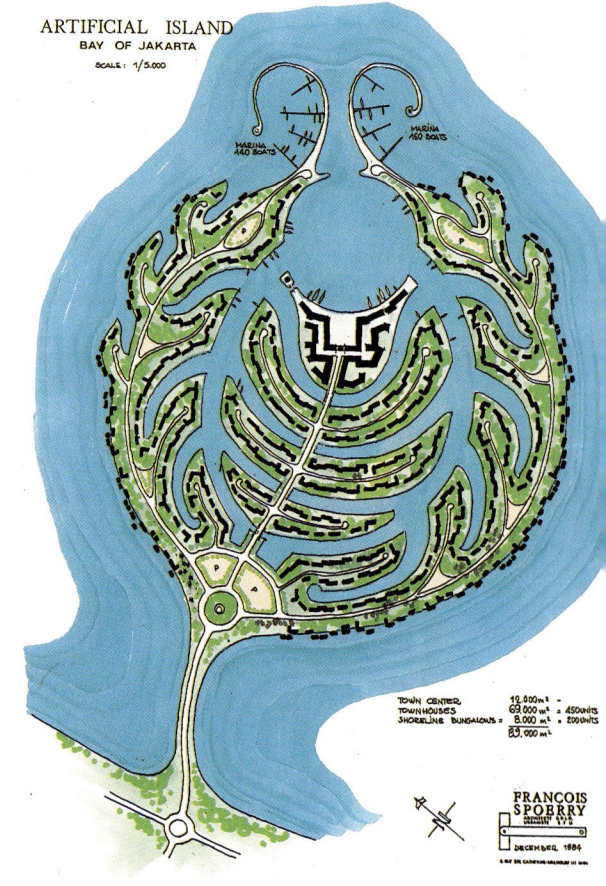

Palmas del Mar, Puerto Rico, 1973. An american developer, who had been captivated by Port Grimaud, commissioned François Spoerry to design him a marina. However, only half of the development was built.

The holiday village of Bendinat is situated on a creek a few kilometres from Palma. The brief compelled us to build a considerable number of houses and apartments upon a fairly small plot of land. We nevertheless had to try to exercise restraint and moderation, and to design buildings which were not going to efface each other. In order to make this plan work, we constructed buildings of modest height amongst the trees. After undertaking an in-depth study of the local architecture and drawing up an extensive inventory with photographs of the local heritage, we tried to create a synthesis directly inspired by the Hispanic tradition with touchs of the Moorish style of Palma and the Balearic Islands.

Bendinat, Palma de Majorca, 1982. The design above was a preliminary sketch scheme, to the right, is a design for the entrance to the village.

In order to build Bendinat's 300 villas and apartments in the midst of such luxuriant vegetation, it was necessary to plan for a high density of buildings to allow sufficient space for the many gardens and areas devoted to leisure pursuits. This, most glamorous and luxurious of villages, was conceived specifically to attract an international clientele to Parma.

At Bendinat, the materials and colours used correspond to those in use in the vernacular architecture of the island. The style of building is very town-like, characterised by the use of cornices, pitched roofs, balconies and iron railings.

The covered verandas, so typical of houses in Palma, where they were used as belvederes, or look-out points in times gone by, are recreated here at Bendinat to form mezzanine floors both giving protection from the heat of the sun and also allowing residents to sleep in the open air.

In the sand dunes six kilometres north of the pyramids, President Sadat had contemplated the possibility of creating new villages in the form of oases, villages in the middle of the desert which would not encroach on adjacent fertile cultivable land. A number of prominent Saudi citizens, anxious to participate in the economic development of Egypt, were associated with this project.

In 1978, in reply to a request from the Egyptian Government, I proposed a plan which called for the use of some of the very oldest of building techniques including, in particular, local material such as clay. In fact, this provided the opportunity to revive much local know-how, for much of the vernacular architecture of the area had been rashly destroyed, a point both exposed by and denounced by the late Hassan Fathy, the historian and architect. We therefore designed these oasis-villages which were closed on their desert side by a continuous frontage of cob dwellings, of one or two floors with terraced roofs – the houses were to form a wall surrounding the village, in the fashion of the fortress villages of the Mediterranean and the Red Sea. This rampart of houses acted as a barrier against the wind, the sand and the scorching sun. Hidden behind it were fountains, gardens, palm trees, secretly held within the many patios and revealed only by the presence of an occasional branch growing from a terrace. The luxuriant vegetation and the abundance of water being made possible by pumping water from the Nile into the oasis-villages. Each quarter was to have its own boutiques, hotels, leisure facilities and shopping centre. From the vantage point of the pyramids these villages, hidden by the sand dunes, remain invisible.

The first disagreements concerned the use of cob, the traditional building material in Egypt. The indigenous population, as well as the wealthy Saudis, who formed the majority of potential clients, made a great outcry, claiming we were trying to make them live in huts like their ancestors. Furious ecologists then added their voices declaring that our aim was to destroy the sacred precincts of the pyramids. A formidable press campaign was launched attacking the project. President Sadat was obliged to bow to the voice of public opinion.

Oasis at the Pyramids, Egypt, 1978. On the edge of the desert, 6 kilometers from the Pyramids, a village was designed to rehouse people from the shanties of the hotter quarters of Cairo. The design of the buildings was inspired by the vernacular architecture of the Nile Valley, their construction was to have been in mud brick.

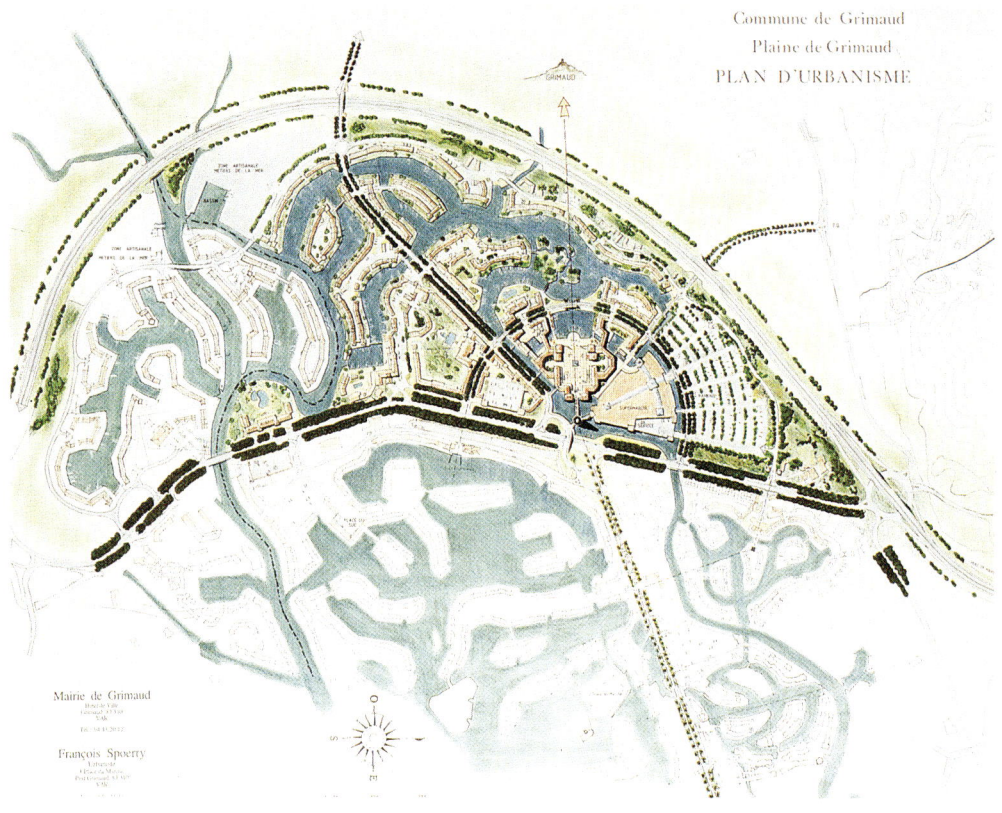

Commune de Grimaud
Plaine de Grimaud
PLAN D'URBANISME

Mairie de Grimaud

François Spoerry

Above an internal courtyard, a small bridge joins the two wings of one of the most sought after large houses in Port Grimaud.

Plaine de Grimaud. The Mayor of Grimaud hopes to restructure the great plain which borders the sea in order to create a fitting frame for the final phase of building at Port Grimaud.

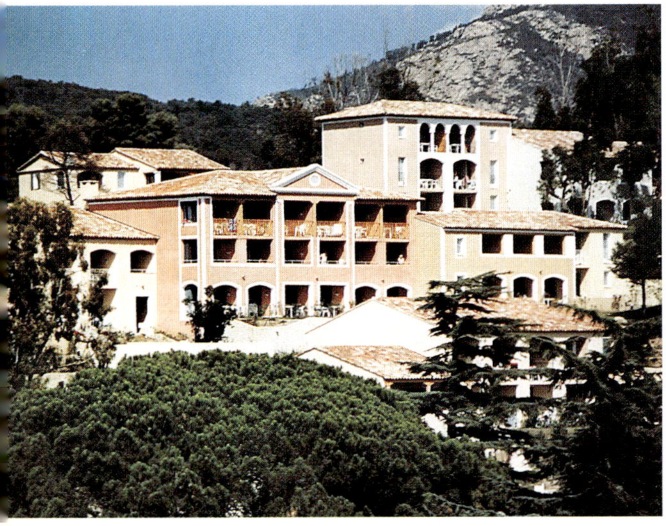

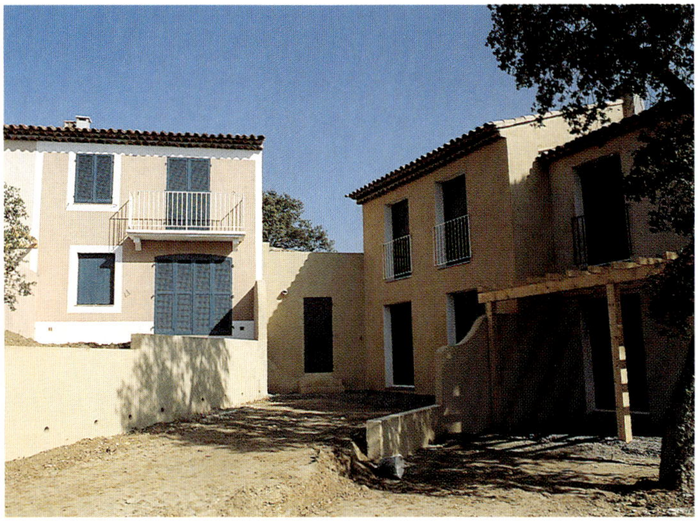

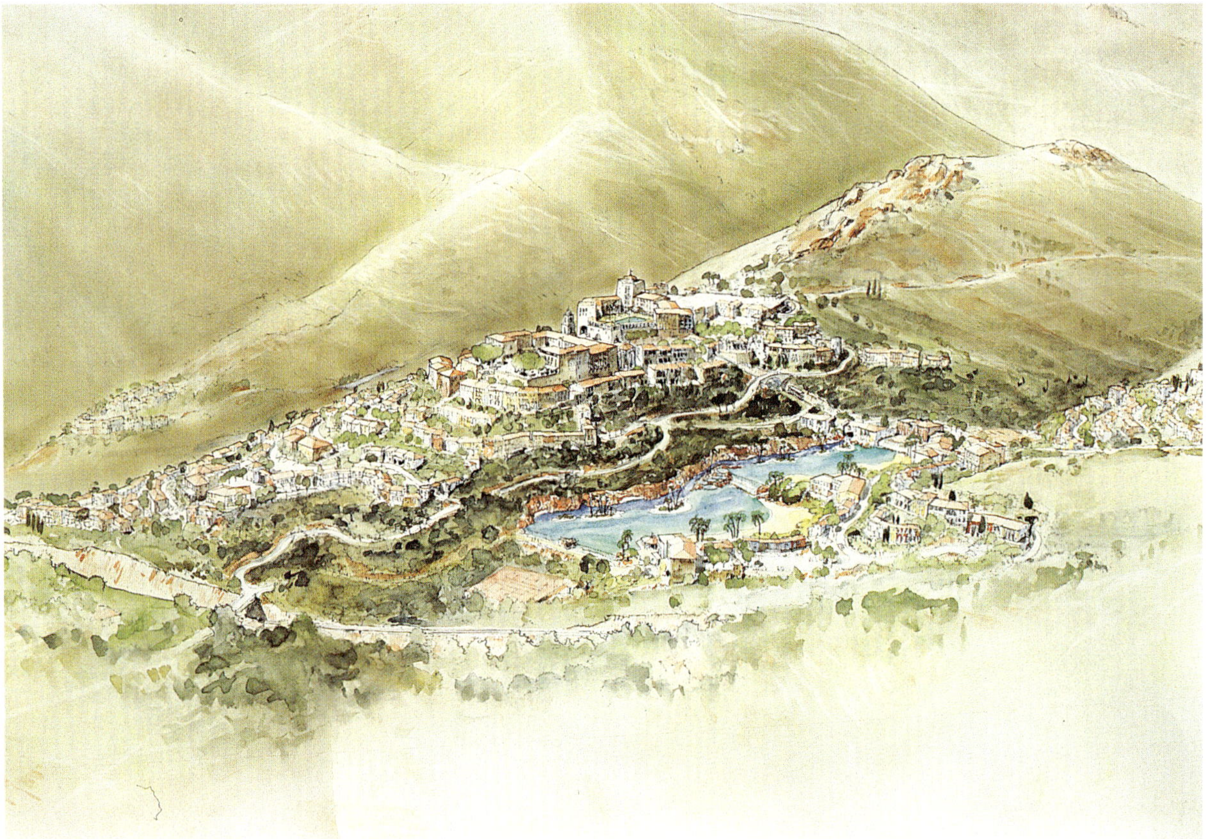

The Grimaud Park (Top far left). While each of the over a hundred studios built on this site is identical, great pains have been taken to ensure that each studio appears individual and different from its neighbours.

Extension to the Village of Gassin (Top near left). This extension has grouped together a hundred detached low-cost houses around a village square together with a number of shops. The very greatest care has been taken not to spoil the character of this listed site.

Eze (Above). Next to this famous village, François Spoerry has designed and built a second village formed by a hotel complex.

Théoule (Bottom left). A major architectural project set on most spectacular headland overlooking the sea.

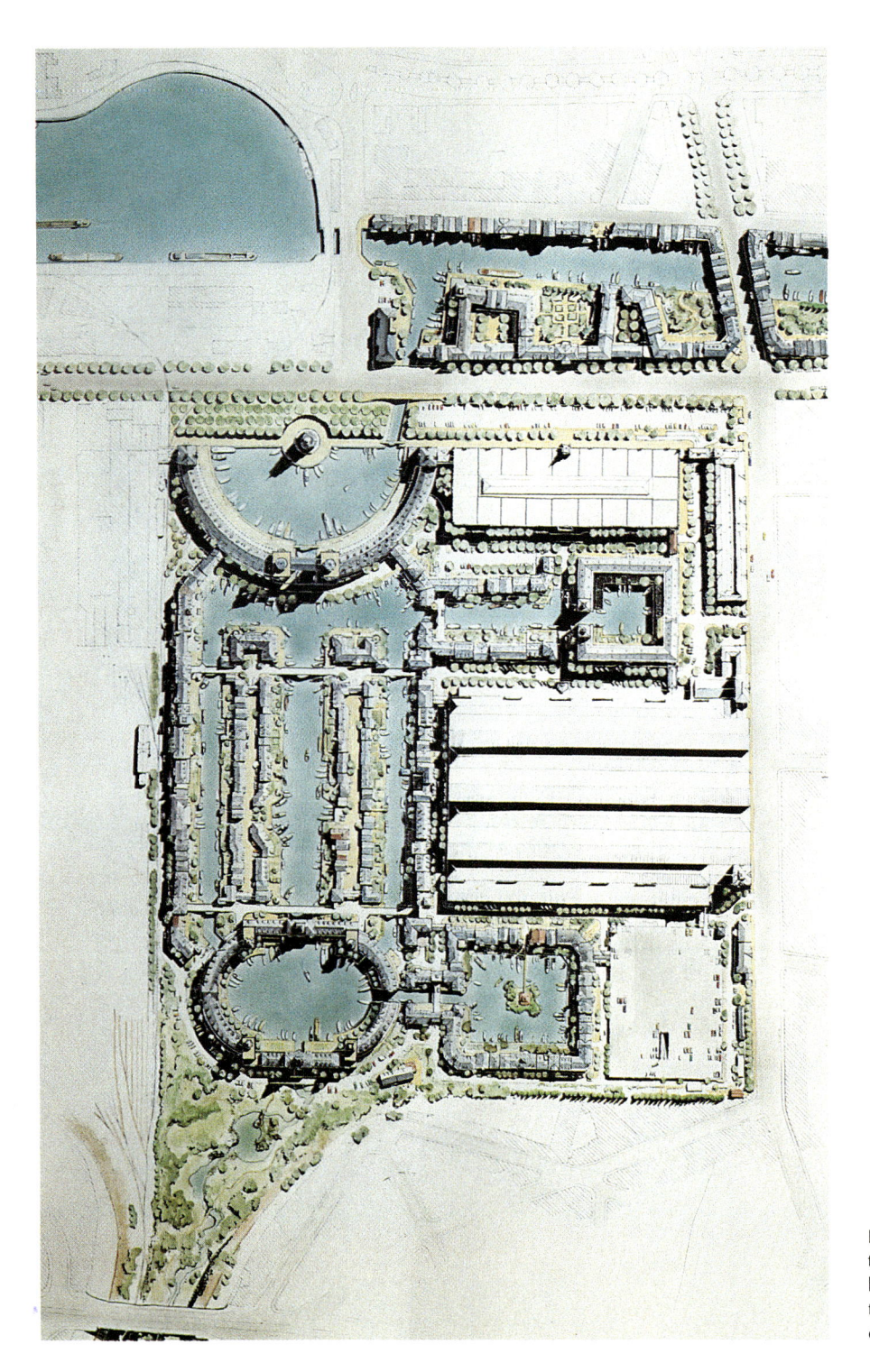

Brussels. A project to transform the site of old marshalling yards bordering a canal which cuts through the city into a dignified complex worthy of a capital city.

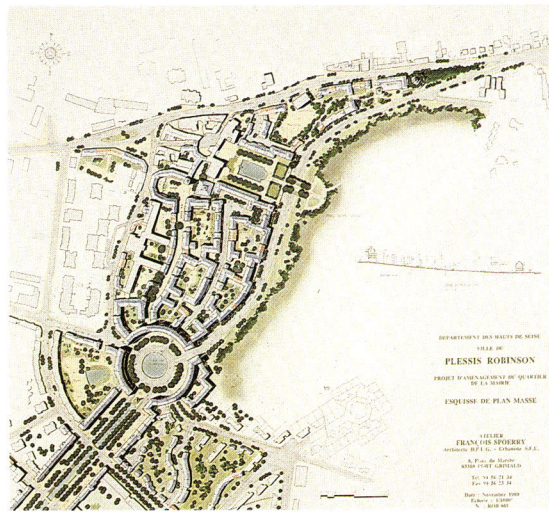

Plessis Robinson. In this ancient commune near Paris, so dominated by d'Artagnan's Castle, the Mayor wants to create a new heart to the town, complete with alley-ways and shops.

TOKYU ARCHITECTS & ENGINEERS
1-1-33 NAKAME-GURO, MEGURO-KU

MIYAKOJIMA ISLAND
OKINAWA-JAPAN

IRIE BAY
LUXURY HOTEL

FRANÇOIS SPOERRY

In the South of Japan, on the Island of Miyako, an important Japanese group have asked François Spoerry to create a small holiday village in the spirit of those of the Côte d'Azur. Pictured here is a view of the magnificent landscaped golf course which only the Japanese know how to create.

A lagoon village on the Inland Sea built in the style of traditional fishermen's houses.

A Great American Project

It was purely by chance that I conceived the idea of Port Liberté. I was having lunch some 430 metres above the ground at the roof-top restaurant of the World Trade Centre in Manhattan, New York. When my gaze wandered rather vaguely over the panoramic view I was struck suddenly by the huge extent of wasteland on the banks of the Hudson River, facing Manhattan. Just a few kilometres from where I was sitting were hundreds of hectares of land, littered with disused wharfs and landing-stages, crumbling warehouses, sheds, hangars, derelict marshalling yards and abandoned railway-tracks. This now desolate stretch of the Hudson river had once been the bustling terminus of the transamerican railways and of the transatlantic shipping companies who loaded and unloaded their cargoes here. But the increasing size of cargoes and the introduction of containerisation had reduced the importance of New York's harbours and so led to the disappearance of bulk cargo handling which was so much slower; gradually these great tracts of land became redundant. As I gazed at this desolate scene, so graphically set against the fabulous backdrop of the Statue of Liberty and Manhattan's incomparable skyline, I had a vision similar to that I had experienced when I first looked upon the barren marshland and sand quarries that were to become Port Grimaud. At that very moment, I visualized the amazing lagoon city that could be built on this vast sad and abandoned site.

Up to this point no developer or architect in New York had shown the slightest interest in these neglected expanses of wasteland. I made a few enquiries as to which sites were available for sale. The one which had the best position was Caven Point, jointly owned by Jersey City and the American Army which had used it as an embarkation port for their "Liberty Ships" in World War II. As soon as I could, I took an option on Caven Point. On my return to France, I made an immediate in-depth study of the project I had in mind. I had made the first detailed scale-model (a risky and expensive business which befalls all architects-cum-developers!) and decided to give my new lagoon city the symbolic name of Port Liberté. I then returned to New York to make a presentation of my model to the Mayor of Jersey City. The mere fact of my having made a detailed study of the project and produced a model immediately raised the value of the waste land on which I hoped to build and which, until I came on the scene, was more of a white elephant than anything else. The whole affair then became very involved and complicated. There was a moment when it seemed as if I were going to be squeezed out of the development of a project which had

Port-Liberté, USA. The open central square on the harbour, is a subtle allusion to the Piazza San Marco in Venice. Ferries, ensuring a direct link with Manhattan, draw alongside the main quay opposite the magnificent flights of steps.

The steep sloping slate-covered roofs with their chimneys, dormer windows and belvederes, the pedimented facades with their stone quoins, the spacious balconies and terraces which are often covered, all form part of the pleasant style of New England.

· CANAL RESIDENCES ·

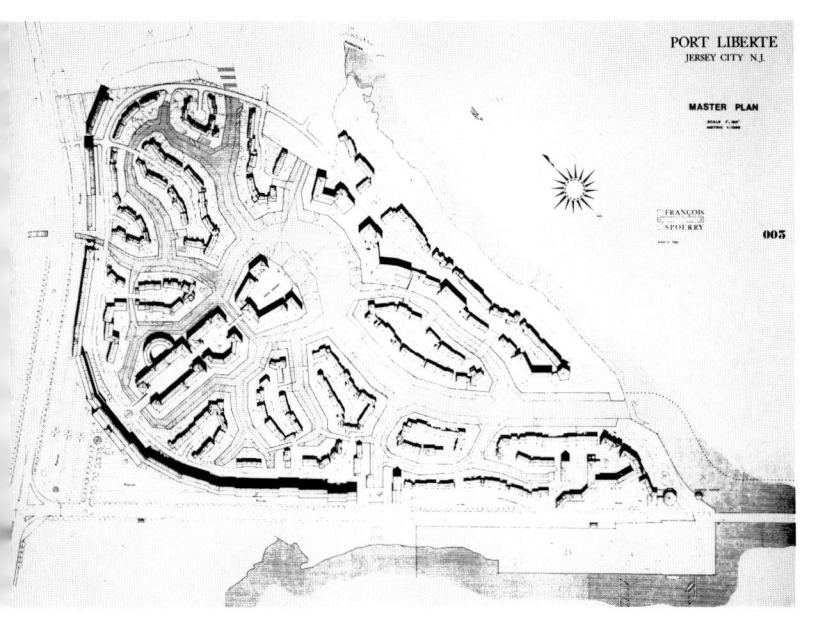

been my idea entirely. However, it was politically unacceptable for the Mayor of Jersey City to sell a sufficient acreage of land on which to build Port Liberté without first inviting American architects to take part in a competition. This meant, of course, that any winning design by an American architect would have cut mine out completely. Forty-five architects took part in the competition, and fourteen different projects were submitted. A jury, wholly independent of City Hall, was formed and, fortunately, my scheme won their vote. I had had a very narrow squeak!

But our problems were not yet over. We still had to find financial partners to help back the development of what was in effect an entire new district of New York, comprising two thousand dwellings, with fifty thousand square metres set aside for office space, as well as a three hundred room hotel, two hundred shops, an impressive number of quays and a web of man-made canals. In around 1850, the town had gradually become cut off from the river. This separation took place at a time when the railways and docks took over the coastal belt then occupied by residential quarters and parks. Taking this into consideration, my project envisaged (up to a certain point) the reconstitution of that long-gone landscape and

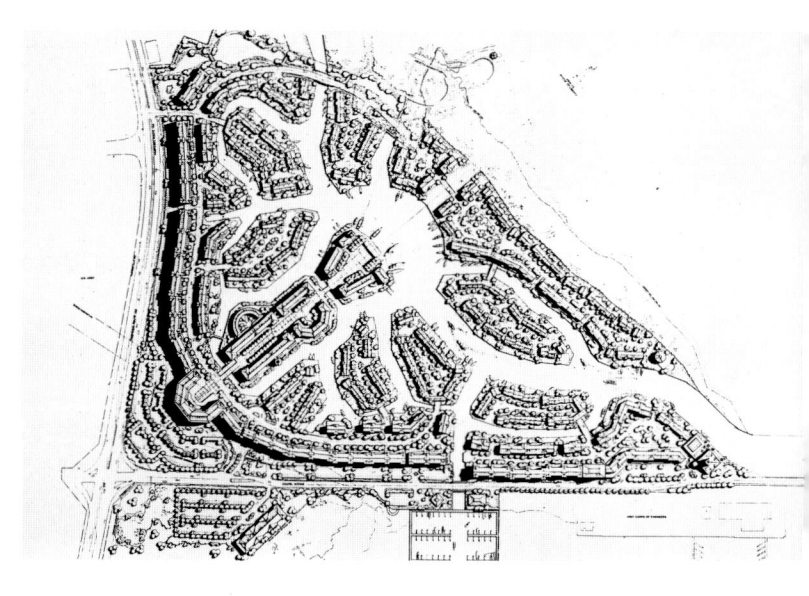

The plans, drawn up in 1984, clearly show a central axis crossing both the shopping quarter and the heart of the town and extending to the Statue of Liberty in the distance. As at Port Grimaud, all the houses benefit from having access both to the canals and to the streets behind.

the restoration of living conditions that had at one time been the norm. Historic documents showed the existence of opulent private residences overlooking the water, gardens and parks, and in keeping with the early Dutch settler's love for ships and the sea, craft moored in close proximity to the houses.

I determined that Port Liberté should reflect some aspects of this picturesque past. The building of a residential complex on the banks of the Hudson River revives an old New York tradition, halted by the large scale commercial development of the port. We devised an interesting approach to town planning which included a girdle, or protective enclosure, around the town. This was to ensure peace and privacy while cutting it off from its surroundings which at present are rather less than attractive. The design as a whole, takes as its focal point the town centre which comprises shops, a first-class hotel, offices and a church all facing the impressive main quay.

I took my inspiration from the local architecture of the towns and villages of New England. All the characteristic architectonic elements of the lovely old houses are used in the buildings of Port Liberté – bow windows, dormer windows, cupolas atop the slate roofs, brick walls with stone quoins, classical columns and pediments, acroters, sash windows, traditional facades with charming front doors in decorative porticoes. This whole neo-classical vocabulary is harnessed, I hope, so as to create an elegant ambiance which is both charming and harmonious .

Port Liberté, built in collaboration with the Ehrkrantz Group of New York, has met with such a warm welcome that preparatory studies are already in progress for further residential and commercial sectors to be developed on the industrial waste lands along the Hudson River. I am delighted to have been responsible for inaugurating the original project – the creation of Port Liberté – which has shown the immense possibilities for the further development and town planning which exist so close to the very heart of New York.

Perspectives of some of the buildings at the town centre, and details of a portico and front door – a whole landscape inspired by the architecture of XVIIIth and XIXth century New England.

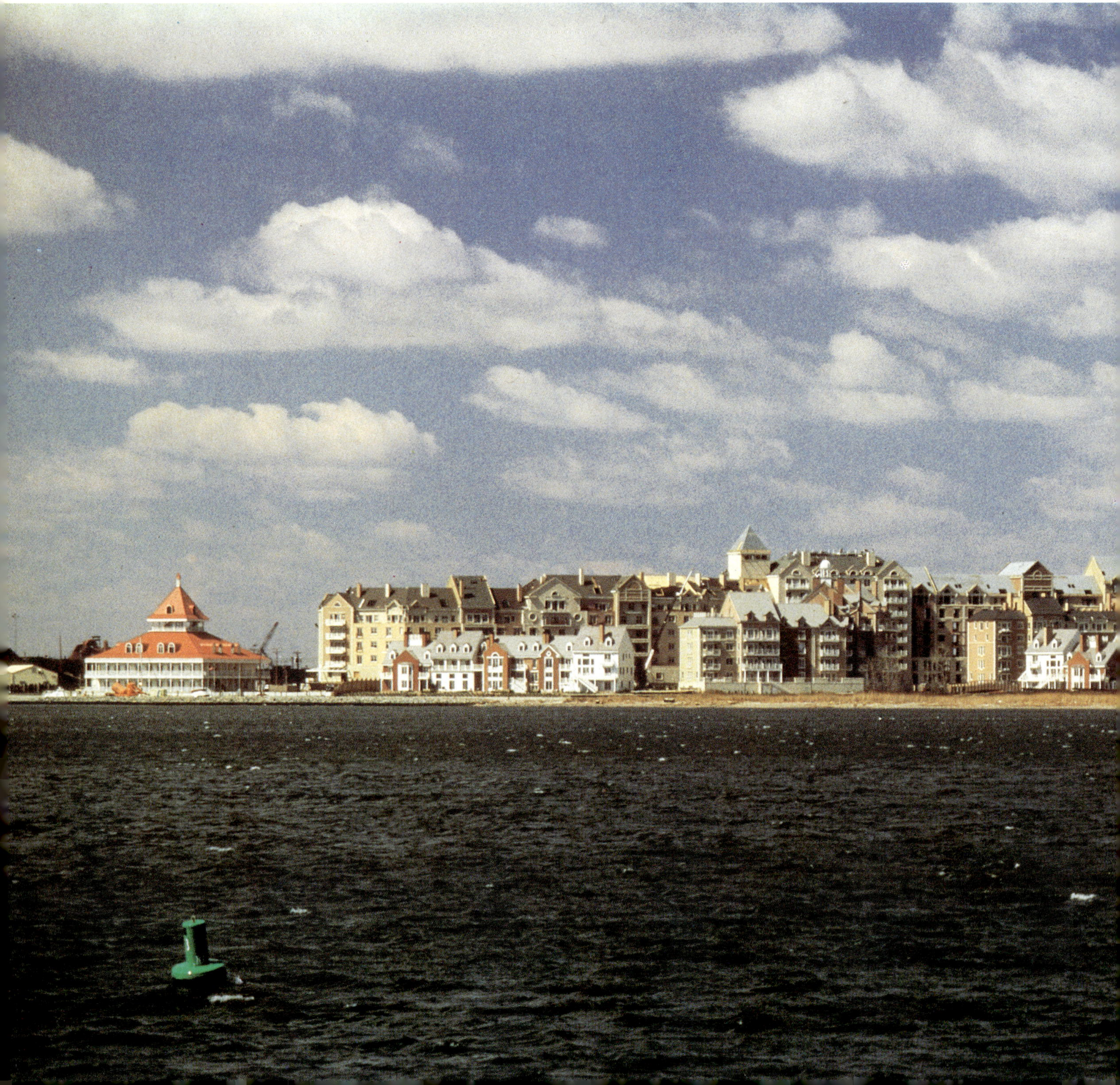

Conceived by François Spoerry four years earlier while having lunch at the top of Manahattan's World Trade Centre, this exciting project for a new town on the water is today's reality, and only a stone's throw from Manhattan itself.

Apartment blocks and individual houses have been built along the excavated canals. Attached to the quays are landing stages enabling all manner of pleasure craft to be moored.

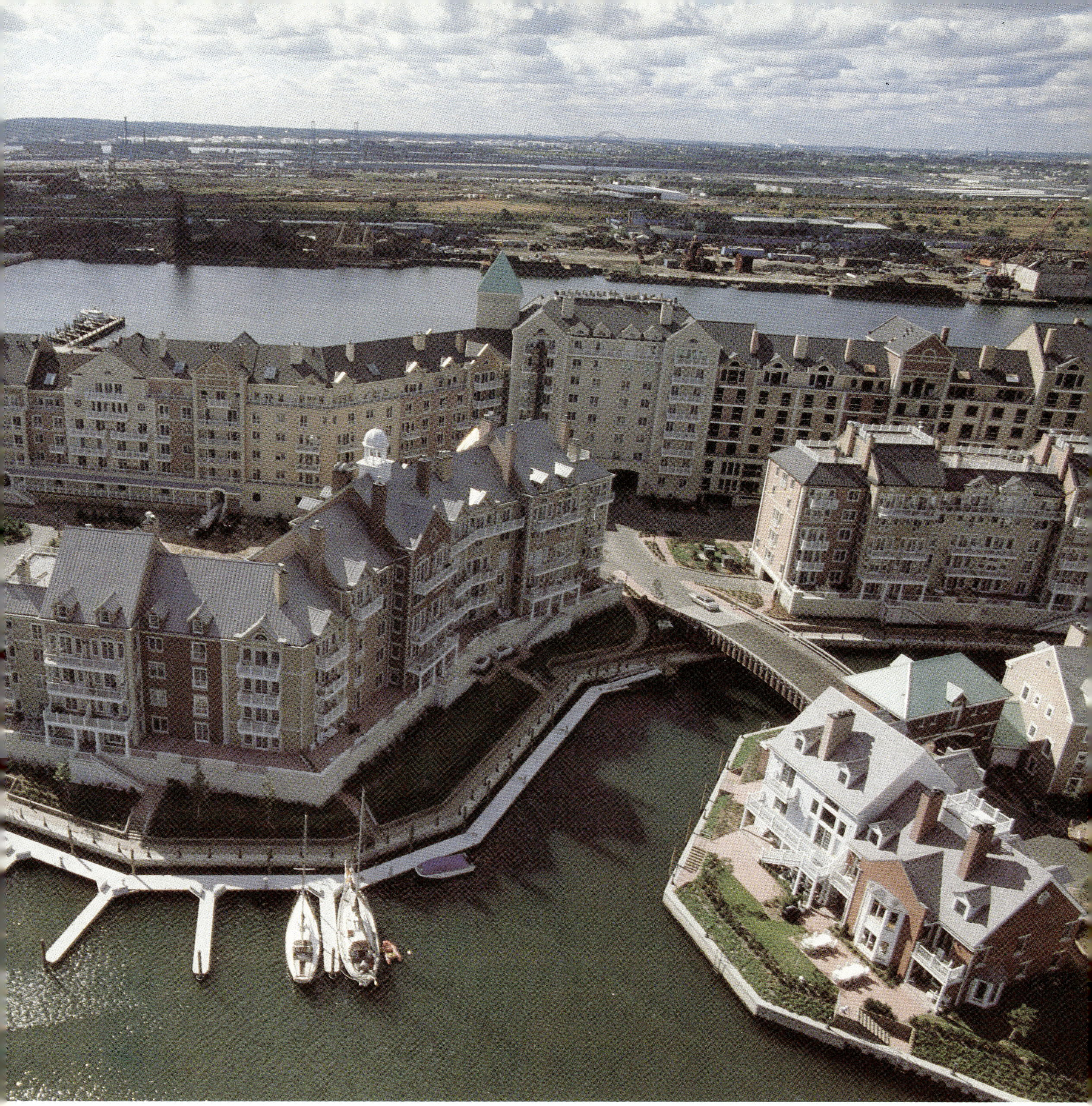

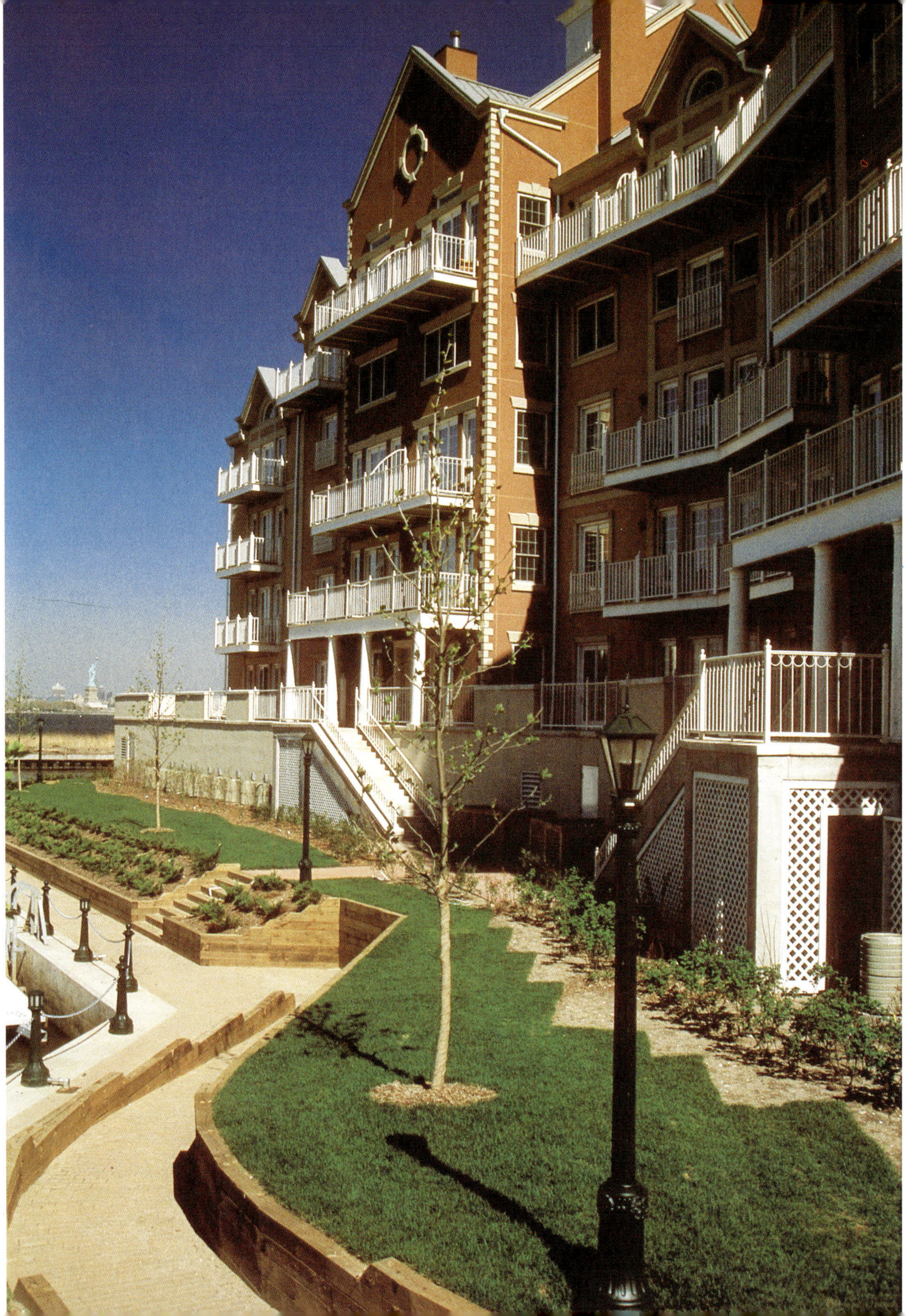

Between the houses and the quays, footpaths and walks have been laid out through the gardens and landscaped areas, all of which are enhanced by the judicious use of street furniture which includes lamp-posts and cast-iron guard railings.

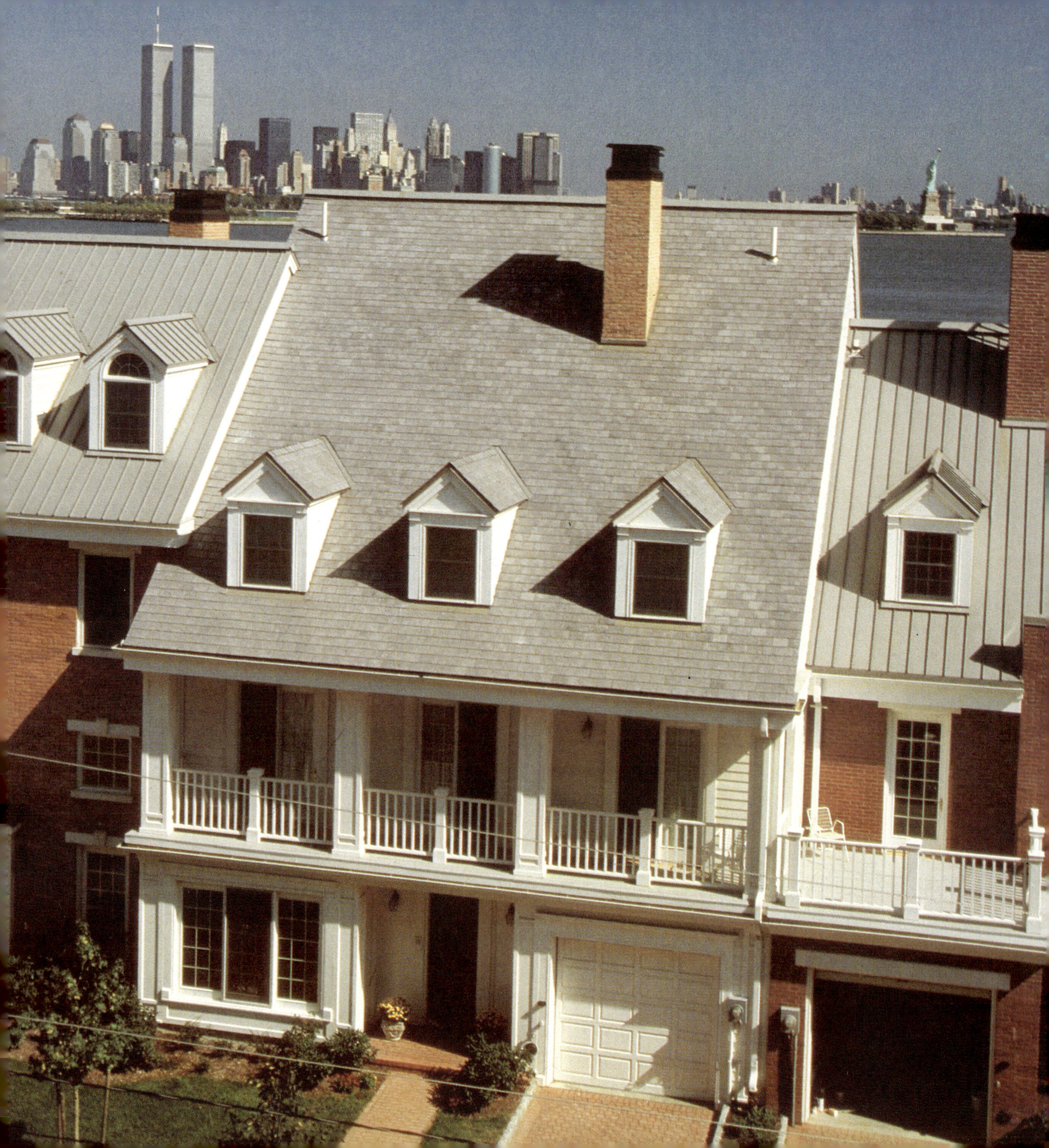

The sky-scrapers of New York, framing the horizon, are in striking contrast to Port Liberté's cheerful houses.

François Spoerry, on a site visit to Port Liberté, pictured standing on one of the wooden bridges in the first quarter to be built.

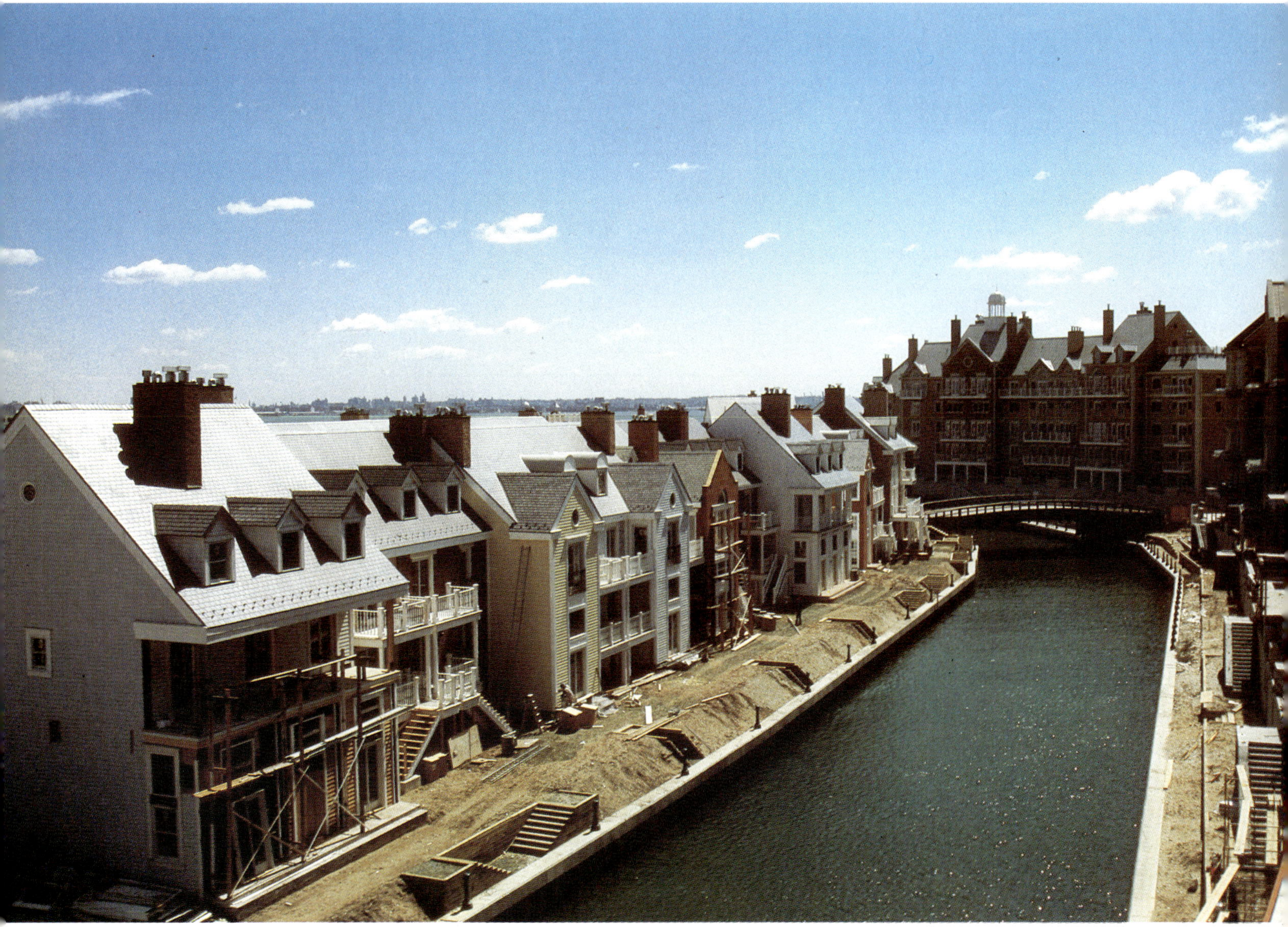

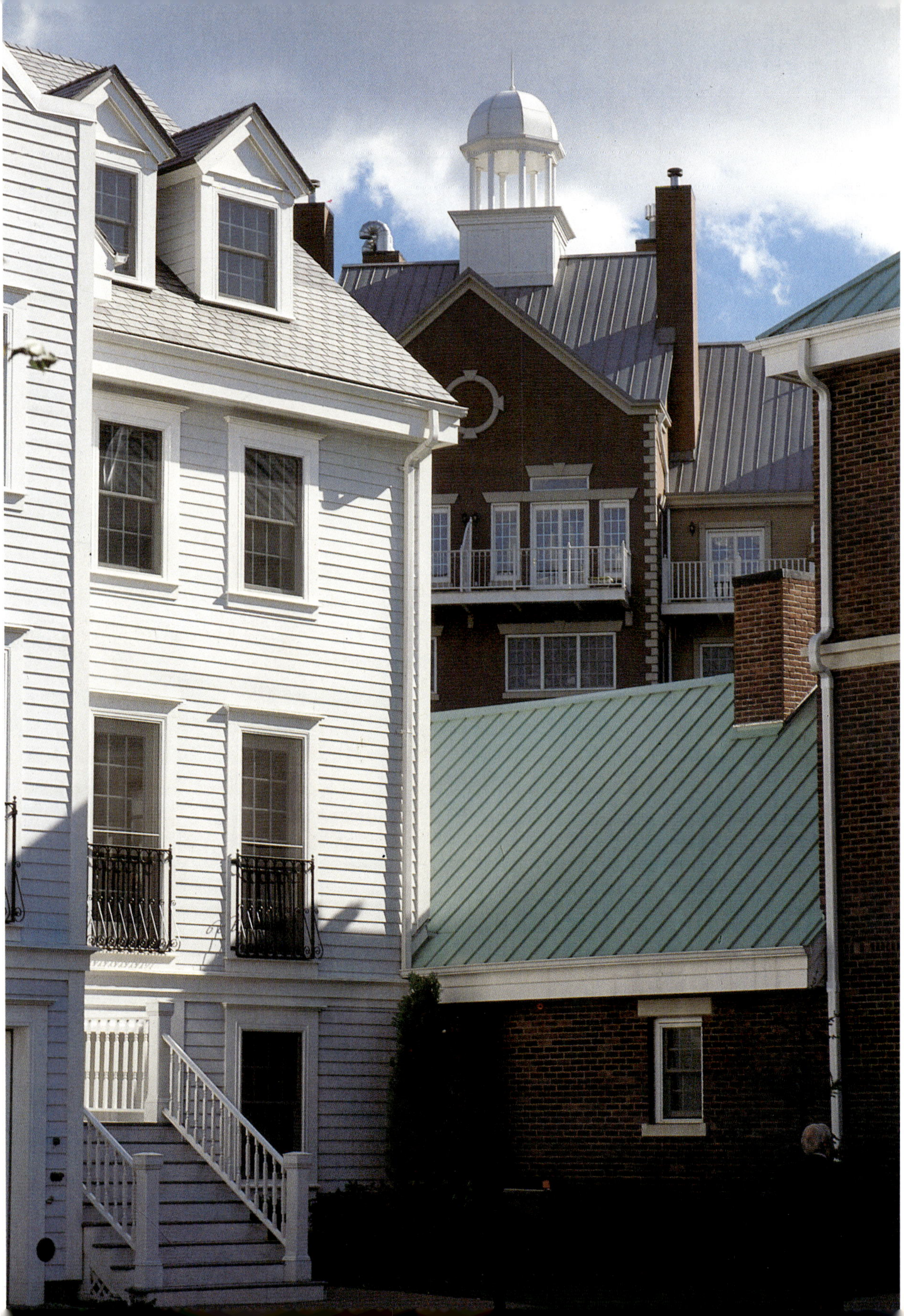

In 1984, the site of a graveyard for old railway engines and carriages, together with the rotting hulks of forgotten liberty ships. Now it is occupied by houses in wood, brick and stucco, the quality of whose details and pastel-coloured facades gives the impression that has never been anything else here but these houses.

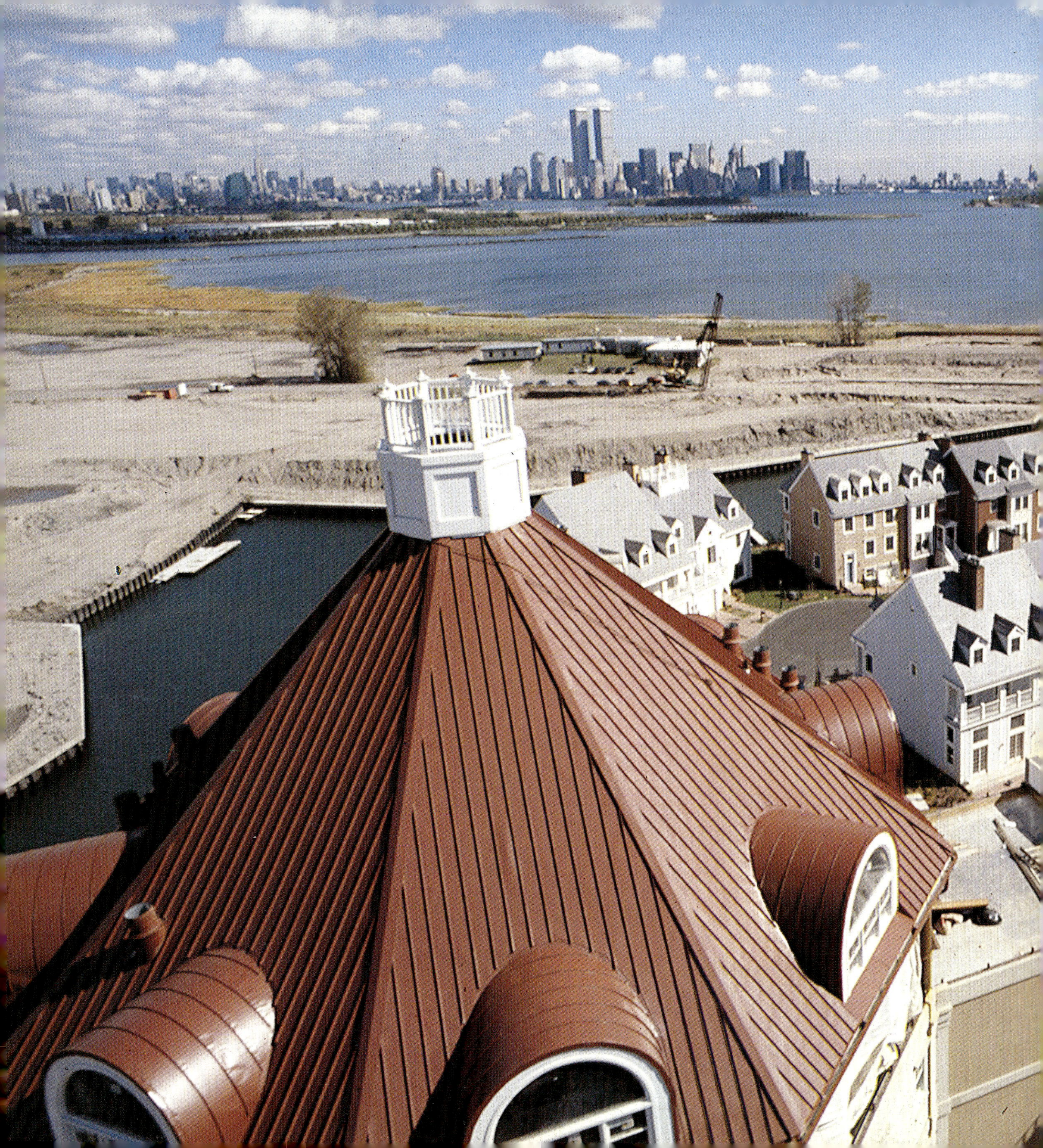

Symbols very dear to Spoerry's heart – The World Trade Centre, The Hudson River, the Statue of Liberty, and in the foreground, Port Liberté in the making.

Architecture Regained

That which is called modern is perhaps that which will not endure.

Dante

Nearly a quarter of a century has elapsed between my having creating Port Grimaud and Port Liberté. This has been a fertile period during which I have learned a good many lessons about lagoons cities most of which were based on my experiences in building Port Grimaud. These have been put into practice elsewhere, whilst always taking into consideration the many differences of climate and topography.

If you ask me what my real goal has been in undertaking these projects, I would say that what I have tried to do is to find a clear connection between popular architecture which varies so very much across the world, and modern architectural technique; to discover common traits, familiar points of reference and to discover the underlying, or the structural, characteristics of cities and villages – these points of reference are neither modern nor ancient, they are timeless.

This is true of all forms of art, but rare indeed are the architects able to handle these new forms artistically. Modern techniques have replaced traditional architectural styles and can be held responsible for spoiling the beauty of both town and countryside. Who today cares about the environment or what can be achieved by overcoming the caprices of climate and topographical obstacles ?

A remarkable exhibition presented in the 60s, *Architecture without Architects,* pointed out that "a fair number of daring and 'primitive' solutions had opened the way to today's cumbersome technology and that many of the 'new' inventions in technology belong in fact to the time honoured school of spontaneous architecture: prefabrication, standardisation of the component parts of flexible or mobile structures, air conditioning, adjustments to lighting and even of lift systems."

As soon as I was in a position to act both as chief workman and chief designer on a project, I put into practice the lessons I had learned when studying the traditional architecture of the cities I visited and which taught me that the quality of life is indivisible from its framework. For me there was no salvation in avant-garde doctrines and in the principles of rationalist town planning. The failure of the great urban complexes was glaringly obvious, as equally was that of "urban renovation" imposed on the suburbs and which resulted in dreary monolithic blocks of concrete high-rise buildings.

How many times have I heard the word "daring" when an architect or town councillor presented one of these projects. *Daring,* the Front de Seine? *Daring,* the Montparnasse Tower? Perhaps I too have sought to be *daring* by turning my back on this style, and on those rules of architectural practice by trying to re-establish harmony and equilibrium in town and countryside by using town planning, historical context, and a sense of continuity.

What then is this particular form of town planning ? Is it not that of giving man back the role we should never have taken from him – that of partner. In the dreary, concrete jungle, devoid of any individual features, its inhabitants have become its prisoners. It is precisely against their captivity that I have rebelled. People are important to me, as is their history, past and present. I have tried to banish stress and anxiety and endeavoured instead to calm and reassure.

In order to accomplish this, I stood aside trying not to impose my ideas with original creations or grandiose and monumental projects, but rather through the use of classic urban forms which, since time immemorial, have represented the traditional town: streets, alleyways and squares, which to its inhabitants speak a known, safe, loved and familiar language.

Ignoring contemporary Promethian visions, I have sought rather to beguile and charm by adapting a variety of architectural and cultural models, such as fountains, *trompe-l'œil*, frescoes, and surprises in the form of a colonnade or an unexpected vista. I have paid particular attention to the treatment of space for both public and private purposes, and I have spoken of "partners" when thinking of the future occupants of a house I was building. It seems to me that this word covers the interaction which is part of the process of seduction. The owner of a property so beguiled will prove my idea of partnership when he takes possession of his new "shell" by the lifestyle he creates within it, by the changes, minimal though they may be, to his front or back garden. He will imprint his personality in a multiplicity of ways, and eventually, he will fulfill my hope that he, his house and his environment will become completely integrated, so that a territory which started out by being the hunting ground of an ideology, becomes a home, a manifestation of the joy of living.

The awareness and statements made by a famous personality across the Channel on matters architectural, and his condemnation of the mistakes committed in London in the last fifty years in the name of Architecture, brought swift and violent reactions. H.R.H. The Prince of Wales followed these statements by appearing in a live television programme in which he boldly attacked the works of established contemporary architects, accusing them of lacking foresight and vision. The main platform of his argument was to point out that modern architecture has sought to conquer nature rather than to work in harmony with it, whereas traditional architecture was always dictated by the local climate and building materials available, by the needs of the inhabitants and by their pleasure in living in pleasant surroundings. In a word, in being close to their past and to their roots.

building materials available, by the needs of the inhabitants and by their pleasure in living in pleasant surroundings. In a word, in being close to their past and to their roots.

The huge concrete buildings dreamed up by town planners find favour only in the eyes of their like-minded fellow architects, but are loathed by the general public... The majority of people in this country have had enough of being lectured by such architects and town planners and being dictated to. The list of disasters for which they are responsible is endless and adds up to the rape of Great Britain.

Following the programme, the *Sunday Mirror* organised an opinion poll which showed that 67% of its readers were heartily in favour of the Prince's opinions, while only 3% did not agree with him. By thus addressing the general public, the controversy took on extraordinary dimensions. So exceptional is the impact of this event that I hardly dare hope that it may mark the dawn of a new age in the history of construction. As the *Economist* wrote, "Prince Charles has forced architecture, that most public but most elitist of the arts, to be vigorously judged and debated; and he has not been ashamed to endorse a few discredited non-economic concepts such as nature, community and – dare he say it – beauty?"

François Spoerry in his studio at
Port Grimaud with one of his
collaborators, Xavier Bohl.

François Spoerry's team from the offices at Port Grimaud and Mulhouse.
From left to right, very back row: Alexandre Couelle, Patrick Sautron, Jacques Repellin and André Canard. *Row 4:* Roger Stoltz, Xavier Bohl, Armand Spiegel, Christine Meyer, Philippe van de Velde and Barbara Stalanq. *Row 3:* Jacques Recoura, Sandrine Giordana, Daniel Barth, Dominique Fagor and Belinda Graf. *Row 2:* Catherine Grege, Frédéric Michelangeli, Gerard Garcia, Fabrice Ricci and Georges Bretones. *Front row:* Pascal Chatillon, Laurent Georges and Michel Riegert.

Chronology

1912	Birth at Mulhouse.
1921 – 1928	Sent to the Lycée at Mulhouse.
1929	An interest in architecture is kindled – design for the family home at Cavalaire.
	Preparation for entry to the School for Naval Cadets at the Lycée St Louis, Paris, but thwarted by the entrance examination.
1930	Preparatory year at the Ecole des Beaux-Arts, Strasbourg.
1932 – 1934	Assistant to the architect, Jacques Couelle.
1935 – 1936	Military Service with the Sappers at Besançon.
1936	Preparation for Ecole des Beaux-Arts, Paris.
1937	Placed first in the entrance examinations for the Ecole des Beaux-Arts at Paris with a study for a wash-house.
	Contestant in the first round, the Twelve Hour Competition of the Prix de Rome, with a study for the Tomb of a Pope.
1939	Charged by the Minister of Education with the mission of producing an inventory of all the principal features and characteristics of the vernacular architecture of the Greek Islands, this involved crossing the Mediterranean by boat in the company of four fellow students.
1939 – 1941	Mobilised at the Declaration of War, saw action on the Somme, and demobilised at Montpellier, he then returned to his home at the Hotel d'Espagnet on the Cours Mirabeau, Aix-en-Provence.
1941 – 1942	Returned to, and completed, his studies at the Ecole des Beaux-Arts at Marseilles in Eugène Beaudouin's studio before becoming a member of the Resistance.
1943 – 1944	Arrested by the Gestapo and transferred first to the Prison of Saint-Pierre at Marseilles and then to Fresnes.
1945	Deported to Germany. Held in a succession of camps which included Buchenwald and Dachau.
	Liberated in May, he then opend his own architect's practice in the rue Sainte-Catherine at Mulhouse.
1945 – 1955	Occupied with the repair of essential war damage as listed in the official files and with the reconstruction of Colmar and Mulhouse.
1957	*Amiens (Nord)* – Conversion and completion of the *Tour Perret*.
1958 – 1960	*Mulhouse (Alsace)* – Realisation of the *Résidence Clémenceau*.
1960 – 1970	*Mulhouse (Alsace)* – Construction of the *Quartier de la place de l'Europe* and the *Tour de l'Europe*.
1963 – 1966	*Port Grimaud (Var)* – Design phase.
1966	*Port Grimaud (Var)* – Construction began on site in June.
1967 – 1975	*Mulhouse (Alsace)* – Building of the residential districts of *d'Entremont* and *Pierrefontaine*.
1971	*Corsica* – Study for the town plan of *Port Diana*.
1972	*Gruissan (Aude)* – Study for a lagoon port.
	Senlis (Val d'Oise) – Competition entry for an extension to the town.
1973	*Puerto Rico* – The partial construction of the *Port of Palmas del Mar*.
	Tunisia – Design study for the Island of Djerba.
1974	*Hyères (Var)* – Design for *la Désirade*.
	Spain – Town planning study for *Port Levant, Costa Brava*.
	Sechal (Alsace) – Town planning study for the thermal spas of five villages.
	Spain – Town planning study for *Puerto Casares*.
1975	*Spain* – Design study for a lagoon port at *Peñiscola*.
	La Rochelle (Charente Maritime) – Design study for a lagoon city.
1976	*Spain* – Town planning study for *Playa Serena, Almeria*.
1977	*United Arab Emirates* – Design study for a marina at *Al Hamriyah*.
	Sardinia – Design for *Porto Cervo* on the Costa Esmeralda which has now been built.
	Haiti – Study for the extension to the city of *Port-au-Prince* to incorporate a marina.
	Ivory Coast – Design study for the Island of Boulay d'Abidjan.
1978	*Hyères (Var)* – Town planning study for the *Lagune des Pesquiers*.
	Egypt – Design study for *Pyramides-Oasis* near Cairo.
	Turkey – Design study for *Port-Kémar* in the Bay of Antalya.
	Corsica – Design for the *Port of Piantarella* near Bonifacio.
1979	*United States of America* – Design study for *Maryland City* at the mouth of the Potomac River.
1980	*Mexico* – Study for a lagoon city at *Puerto Careyes* on the West Coast of Mexico.
1981	*Sardinia* – New commission for *Porto Cervo* on the Costa Esmeralda – this has now been built.
	United States of America – Design for *Port Louis, Louisiana* – in the course of construction.
1982	*The Caribbean* – Design study for *Puerto San Francisco* on the Island of Cozumel.
	The Bahamas – Design study for *New Providence*.

Spain – Design study for the village at *Bendinat, Palma, Majorca* – this has now been built.

1983   *Gassin (Var)* – Designs for an extension to the existing village comprising a school, low cost housing and a golf course – under construction.

1984   *Mexico* – Design study for *Puerto Escondido* – under construction.

Mexico – Study for a lagoon city at *Cancún.*

Indonesia – Project for an man-made island at *Jakarta.*

United States of America – Design of *Port Liberté* – completed.

1986   *France* – Design study for *Port Léman* on Lake Geneva.

Gassin (Var) – Initial designs for *Marines de Gassin* – in the course of realisation.

Grimaud (Var) – Initial designs for *Parc de Grimaud* – in the course of realisation.

1987   *Hyères (Var)* – New commission for *la Désirade.*

Cogolin (Var) – Project for the extension of the village.

Port-de-Bouc (Bouches-du-Rhône) – Initial designs for this project – now under construction.

La Ciotat (Bouches-du-Rhône) – Project for the extension of the port.

Spain – Designs for a threefold project at *Vilaricos* – under construction.

England – Project for the Naval Base on the Thames at *Chatham.*

Spain – Project for *Puerto Nuevo, Santa Pola.*

The Bahamas – Study for *Sandy Port, Nassau* – under construction.

1988   *Mer-Suèvres (Loir et Cher)* – Designs for an extension to a village centered on a golf course.

Roquebrune-sur-Argens (Var) – Study for a village at the centre of a golf course – under construction.

French West Indies – Study for *Port Lisa, St Martin.*

1989   *Gassin (Var)* – Design of a hotel complex, the *Mas de Chastelas.*

Théoule (Alpes-Maritimes) - Design for a village de crête de *Miramar Figueirettes* comprising houses, a tourist centre and shops.

Grimaud (Var) - An apartment block to house 10 flats in a low-cost housing scheme on behalf of the Office d'HLM du Var - under construction.

Porto Vecchio (Corsica) – Study for a lagoon city.

Grimaud (Var) – Design for a residential complex, *Les Restanques.*

Plessis-Robinson (Région Parisienne) – Design for the creation of a town centre.

Roquefort-les-Pins (Alpes-Maritimes) – Design for a complex to include a hotel and holiday accomodation.

Sanary (Var) – Conversion of the sea-front esplanade.

Saint Pons (Var) – Designs for a lagoon complex of housing and shops in the vicinity of Port Grimaud.

Mulhouse (Alsace) – Design of *Le Charles X,* a luxurious block of flats and offices – in the course of completion.

Golf du Manoir Souffleheim (Alsace) – Design for a residential and hotel complex around a golf course.

Altkirch (Alsace) – Main dwellings for *La Closeraie* – now built.

Riedisheim (Alsace) – A complex of homes and shops known as *Le Clos de la Seigneurerie* – being built.

Hirsingue (Alsace) – An apartment block known as *La Colombière* – being built.

Germany – Design study for a lagoon city on an island in the Elbe near Hamburg.

Spain – Design study for a residential and hotel complex at *Punta Negra, Majorca.*

Japan – Design for two holiday resorts on the *Island of Miyako,* comprising hotels, houses and shops.

1990   *Bassussarry, near Biarritz (Pyrénées Atlantiques)* – Design for a residential complex surrounding a golf course.

Port Chiberta (Pyrénées Atlantiques) – Project to create a port at the mouth of the Adour to include housing, shops and a leisure centre in a new quarter of the town.

Eze (Alpes Maritimes) – Project to create a hotel and residential complex next to the village.

Vitrolles (Bouches-du-Rhône) – Design for a residential complex with shops around a lake.

Puyricard (Bouches-du-Rhône) – Design for a residential complex in the Commune of Aix-en-Provence.

Ventabren (Bouches-du-Rhône) – Project for 16 detached houses near Aix-en-Provence.

Le Ginestel (Var) – Project for the future development of the Plain of Grimaud.

Bellème (Orne) – Design for 185 holiday lodges around a golf course.

Morlaas at Cagnes-sur-Mer (Alpes Maritimes) – Project for a complex of 45 homes as principal residences.

Le Perrussier at Roquebrune-sur-Argens (Var) – Design for a residential complex linked to a golf course.

Portugal, Vilamoura, Algarve - Design for a lagoon city.

Spain, Bendinat, Majorca, The Polygon Centre - Design for a residential and hotel complex with its own shopping area built around a golf course.

Japan – Project to convert the Bay of Sagami for Surf 90.

Finland – Design for a small village in vernacular style.

St-Paul-en-Forêt (Var) – Project for a complex of main residences, second homes, holiday homes and a hotel.

Complementing his *Gentle Architecture,* Spoerry even invented a small car, the *"Minicar"*, which was patented in 1975. This tiny car-about-town is fitted with an electric motor. It can park at right angles to the pavement. Because it is front opening, one can step directly onto the pavement. Its four wheel steering, controlled by two super-imposed steering wheels, makes driving in cities an absolute joy.

Index to the photographs and illustrations

Bendinat, 89–92
Brussels, 98
Cancún, 78–79
Cogolin, 70
Djerba, 86
Eze, 97
Gassin, 70, 96
Gruissan, 65
Jakarta, 88
La Ciotat, 72
La Désirade, 68
Les Parc de Grimaud, 96
Mer-Suèvres, 71
Miyako Island, 100–101
Mulhouse, 29–31
Palmas del Mar, 88

Plaine de Grimaud, 94–95
Plessis Robinson, 99
Port de Bouc, 71
Port Grimaud, 33–59, 94–94, front end papers
Port Levant, 86
Port Léman, 74–75
Port Liberté, 102–119, rear end papers
Port Lisa, 87
Port Louis, 76
Puerto Careyes, 86
Puerto Escondido, 80–85
Pyramid-Oasis, 93
Roquebrune sur Argens, 73
Senlis, 68
Théoule, 96
Vilaricos, 87

Notes and incidental remarks

Clough Williams Ellis was something of a maverick. He was born in 1883 and after attending Oundle and Cambridge he embarked with unflagging panache and verve on an imaginative and controversial career as an architect which was to span the reign of the many British monarchs from Victoria to Elizabeth. At Stowe he converted a neglected country house into a new public school and on his own home ground continued to distill the architectural essence of the Mediterranean to grace his private peninsula on the North Wales coast where he had created an elegant setting for holidays and conferences much beloved of artists and writers. Portmeirion's praises have been sung by many admirers including modernist architects of the strictest rectitude.

Clough Williams Ellis crusaded for the National Parks, the National Trust, the Councils for the Protection of Rural England and Wales, and many other bodies concerned with conservation and good planning. His work covered every aspect of architecture from the restoration of stately homes to the entire planning and rebuilding of London's Battersea Dogs' Home and of country quarantine quarters. He died in 1978 leaving the world a poorer place; for men like Clough Williams Ellis are rare and special people.

photographic credits

Laurent Bianquis, 126; Éric Brissaud, 106-107, 108-109, 113 (upper), 114 (lower), 116, 118-119, rear end papers; Collection Marc Gaillard, 25 (upper), 26; Claude Gaspari, 14, 36-37, 38 (lower), 39, 40, 41, 46, 47, 50, 51, 52-53, 54, 55, 57 (right), 59 (lower), 64-65, 67, 72, 78, 80, 81, 83, 114; Geay Aero - La Bocca, front end papers; Gérard Guillat, 27; Heim de Balsac - Paris, 68; Claude Lemoin, 113 (lower), 117; Georges Palot - Paris, 25 (lower); Raymond - Nice, 20 (upper right); Studio Jean-Paul - Guebwiller, 31; Transacphot - Grasse, 33. All other photographs are from the personal collection of François Spoerry (All Rights Reserved).

Typeset by Carden Publications limited.
Printed in France by Ouest Impressions Oberthur, Rennes.
Photogravure by Prodima-Bilbao, Spain.
ISBN 0 471 93086 5 (England)   ISBN 2 221 05450 4   (France).

The rights of François Spoerry to be identified as the author of this work have been asserted in accordance with ss. 77 and 78 of the Copyright, Designs and Patents Act 1988.

No part of this publication may be reproduced, stored in a retrieval system, or transmitted in any form, or any means, electronic, mechanical, photocopying, photographic, recording, or otherwise, without the express written permission of John Wyley & Sons Ltd.